SEÁN MAC RÉAMOINN

The Synod on the Laity
An Outsider's Diary

the columba press

the columba press

8 Lower Kilmacud Road, Blackrock, Co Dublin, Ireland.

First edition 1987
Cover designed by Bill Bolger
Origination by Typeform Ltd, Dublin
Printed in Ireland by
Mount Salus Press, Dublin

ISBN 0 948183 52 7

Contents

Teicht do Róim:
Mór saído, becc torbai!
In rí chondaigi hi foss,
Manimbera latt, ní fogbai.

To come to Rome:
Great labour, little gain!
The King you seek you won't find here,
Unless you bring him with you.

(Irish: 9th Century)

Preface

This is in every sense of the word an 'outsiders' account of the 1987 Synod. Although I have reported on several of these assemblies I have never been inside the Synod Hall, I am a member of no church committee or organisation, Irish or international, and I am certainly no Vaticanologist. So, for any and all errors and omissions I can only plead, with Dr. Johnson, 'Ignorance . . pure ignorance'. . .

   To Michael, Pauline and Robin who sheltered and fed me, and to Julia and Tony who minded me, I dedicate these pages, which they are under no obligation to read. And to all my Roman friends and benefactors: *mille grazie, míle buíochas!*

S. MacR.

Prologue

Dublin, Thursday, 24th September
This afternoon I attended a news conference in the Catholic Press and Information Office in Booterstown. The usual suspects from the media were there, but also the great and good Nuala Kernan and Maureen Groarke, chairman and secretary of the Irish Bishops' Commission for the Laity, with some of their colleagues – as indeed the occasion demanded. For we had been summoned by Jim Cantwell, who runs the Office, to meet Cardinal Tomas Ó Fiaich, Archbishop of Armagh and Primate of All Ireland, along with Bishop Cahal Daly of Down and Connor, prior to their setting out for Rome and the Seventh General Assembly of the Synod of Bishops, as representatives of the Irish Bishops' Conference.

The subject of the Synod is, as every altar boy (and girl) should know, *The Vocation and Mission of the Laity in the Church and the World, twenty years after the Second Vatican Council.* And it's due to begin a week from today, on 1st October.

Both cardinal and bishop were, as ever, friendly and helpful, but had little to add to their joint statement. The Irish written submission to the Synod is still, apparently, under wraps and, asked what they were going to say when they got there, they not unreasonably replied that they'd wait and hear what speakers before them say, in order to avoid the repetitive proclamation of agreed opinions, which can be such a wasteful and boring feature of such assemblies. But they would stress the need for partnership between bishops, priests and people; a stronger role for women; and urgent problems of social justice, which the laity could do much towards solving . . . Yes: the sixty non-episcopal 'auditors' (nearly all of them lay men and women) who are to attend the Synod could and would take part in the proceedings (but without voting powers). No: the one Irish name among them – Mr Patrick Fay of the Legion of Mary – had not been chosen or proposed by the Irish Bishops, though the Cardinal *had* made another proposal . . . No: neither the Cardinal nor the bishop would be bringing 'advisers', lay or clerical, to Rome.

And that seemed to be that. Until a few minutes ago when I rang the office to check something, I learned that after I'd left Booterstown, the Cardinal announced quite informally that he was personally inviting Ms Kernan and Ms Groarke (the great and good previously mentioned). And a very good thing too. I hope they can accept: it did seem quite appalling that not even the executives of the bishops' own laity commission would be next or near an assembly called to discuss, of all things, the vocation and mission of the laity. The fact that the two individuals in question, who will now be there, however unofficially, are women is an added bonus. One up for the Cardinal!

Preparations

A bit of good news like that doesn't come amiss. For I must say that my own mood of mild pessimism about the Synod seems to be shared by most of those interested enough to discuss it with me in recent times. Perhaps I know the wrong kind of people.

Or perhaps it's an illustration of the Irish maxim *an rud a théann i bhfad, téann sé i bhfuaire.* * The preliminaries for the Synod seem to have been going on for ever and things do feel a bit chilly. Back in 1985, a rather inadequate press notice asked for suggestions as a matter or urgency, but then most of us heard nothing for some months. It is no criticism of the Cardinal or Bishop Daly to take their statement that 'in preparation for the Synod extensive consultations were carried out in Ireland, at local, diocesan and national level' with perhaps just a very small grain of blessed salt. For while it is literally true that 'extensive consultations' *were* held here and there (not least, I understand, in the authors' own dioceses), it was a very spotty affair indeed. Even the efforts of the Laity Commission (to whom tribute is justly paid) were not enough to break through the widespread torpor. And, of course, some at least of the blame must be laid at the ghostly door of our non-existent consultative structures.

Not that the document on which consultation was to be based was of much help. This was known as the *Lineamenta*, a rather woolly confection of questions issued by the Synod secretariat to, in the first instance, the various episcopal conferences, but clearly intended for wider circulation – and equally clearly not very suitable for the purpose. As the Cardinal told us, he felt obliged to paraphrase it, and

*'What's prolonged grows cold.'

12

similar action was taken by other bishops – and, I understand, the Laity Commission.

But however inadequate this working paper, and however limited the consultation, replies and comments did come in and were duly 'processed'. To what extent they influenced or affected the Irish episcopal submission in reply to the *Lineamenta,* or indeed what was the content or thrust of that reply, can only be guessed at, as the bishops considered themselves strictly bound to secrecy – and, as has been indicated above, still do. An honourable proceeding, but not very encouraging to those not closely involved.

Pobal

At this stage I must 'declare an interest'. In April 1986 a few of us here in Dublin felt we should try to get more people thinking about the whole matter, on a country-wide basis; to bring those interested together to express their beliefs and opinions, and ultimately to publish these and bring them to the attention of the Synod itself.

A first one-day consultation of some fifty people, invited more or less at random from all over the country, encouraged us to go on. The second stage was the publication of a volume of essays, by lay and clerical writers, under the title of *Pobal* (from *Pobal Dé,* the traditional Gaelic name for God's People)*. As we said in the foreword, it was 'unashamedly a book with a message . . . to the Irish Catholic Laity, in order to alert their interest in the Synod.' We pointed out that as things stood, the voice of the laity would be heard there 'only indirectly, if at all'. And, we added, 'the ideas and enactments of the Synod are unlikely to make any direct impact on ordinary Catholics'. The book was an attempt 'to do something about it'; it includes biblical and historical studies as well as reflections on the current scene.

As a follow-up, the hoped-for wider gathering of 'ordinary, interested Catholics' did eventually take place in March of this year. Over two hundred lay men and women, of varying ages and backgrounds, attended, some indeed representing their parishes. They came 'to think, to argue, to pray, to think again and finally to proclaim'. All this they did and what they heard and said and thought can be read in *Lay People in the Church: Papers of the Pobal Conference.* (Dominican Publications, Dublin, 1986).

* *Pobal: The Laity in Ireland,* ed. Mac Réamoinn, Columba Press, 1986.

Instrumentum Laboris

That was six months ago. Since then nothing much has happened, in public any way. There have been a few pronouncements, by far the most interesting of which was an address given by Denis Carroll, Dublin curate and theologian, to a one-day conference organised by the Laity Commission. The conference was not open to the public, but enough of the address was reported to make one eager to read it. It will in fact be published before this Diary sees the light *(Doctrine and Life,* October 1987), so I'll say no more about it, though I may have a quote or two later.

But if Ireland has been inactive, the Synod secretariat has clearly been busy, because summer brought us the *Instrumentum Laboris,* the second discussion document, described officially as 'a kind of collection resulting from an analysis of the reflections, experiences, suggestions and proposals' made by those to whom the earlier *Lineamenta* had been circulated – and, less officially, given the rather unkindly title of 'Laborious Instrument'!

Unkindly, and not altogether fair. For while a bit stretched and windy in places, one should remember that it is a *compilation,* in which many minds and hands have had a part – indeed, as such, it is remarkably homogeneous in tone: and it does contain a lot of solid stuff.

Without access to the texts of the various submissions on which the document is said to be based, it is impossible to say whether all those consulted were remarkably united, not to say uniform, in their ideas on the subject. Or whether editing meant 'homogenisation' – involving, in some cases, simple suppression. I hope that the actual synodal discussions will reveal a livelier pluralism.

Certain statements seem, to say the least of it, rather odd. For instance:

> Marriage gives a particular importance to the state in life of the majority of the laity. It indeed confers on the lay state a supernatural character which is not attainable in other states. . .
> Since the family is the domestic Church, then the intimate *communio* of life and love, the relationship of husband and wife, of paternity and maternity, of offspring and fellowship which are born in it, ought to become the aim of the laity's mission . . . (par 29)

Again:

> The parish continues to be the usual place of participation by the

laity in the Church's life and mission. In parishes they discover and constantly live their character as people of God . . . (par 57). The family is of decisive importance in the proper wellbeing of the person and for the soundness of the social framework. Through family life animated from the perspective of Christian holiness, the laity are able to transform daily life and render it more beneficial to the human person both in urban and rural areas. (par 65)

As I have noted elsewhere, of these propositions the second and third are arguable, but questionable in point of fact: the first I find hard to make any sense of. The best that can be said of it is that it represents a well-intentioned but confused attitude to the dignity of marriage, at the expense of other 'states of life'.

On the other hand, the document discusses a number of fundamental questions with perception and clarity: 'the distinction between vocation and mission'; 'the relation existing among the *Church*, the *world*, and the *kingdom of God*'; 'mission' and the 'mystery of evil'. And there are some splendid observations on a variety of matters:

The Church cannot be a partner to darkness . . . (par 21)

The experience of living in modern society places many lay people under a tremendous tension between Christian values and the contra-values of the world. The result for them is two opposing temptations: to seek refuge in forms of religion without substance, constituting a flight from the world; or to reject the demands of Christian faith in order to conform to a worldly existence. (ibid)

A sceptical attitude to politics has no reasonable foundation among Christians. (par 69)

No area of human life or activity can be untouched by the Christian presence. (par 63)

In the mass-media field the laity must be defenders of freedom, respect for the dignity of the human person and the growth of an authentic culture of peoples . . . (par 68)

All well said, but one might ask why specify 'lay people' or 'laity' in the second and fifth of these quotations? Surely the 'tension between Christian values and the contra-values of the world' and the qualities needed in relation to the mass media apply to all Christians (except, possibly, some strictly enclosed religious)?

Dualism

And so I come to my main problem with the *Instrumentum* and, indeed, with the Synod itself. I mean that 'clerical-lay' diochotomy or duality which seems to be close to the very core of pre-Synod thinking, as expressed in this paper, but also in many other documents and addresses, at home and abroad.

I am far from suggesting that this is something new, still less a synodal invention. To one brought up in the years between the wars, the two God-given classes of Irish society seemed to be clergy and laity. I can remember scores of reports in the local papers describing how some civic function, *tabhairt amach,* or bunfight 'attracted a large and distinguished attendance of clergy and laity'. The event in question was not at all necessarily of an ecclesiastical or religious nature . . . however secular the occasion, the two classes must be mentioned. In another time and another place, the reference might have been to 'nobility, gentry and' – perhaps – 'respectable tradesmen'! Indeed it is tempting to see the later usage as a substitute and successor . . . rather as calling a bishop 'My Lord!' seemed to satisfy an old hunger for forelock-touching. But I think it goes deeper than that: certainly the Gaelic usage *cléir agus tuath* seems deeply rooted, and in no way dependent on what we like to call 'alien influences'.

On the other hand, I believe it is an over-simplification to equate 'clergy-laity' with 'priest and people'. The latter could clearly be seen as expressing an omnipresent social reality of function – as transparent as those involving the doctor, the teacher, the tailor, the blacksmith (and his successors). But 'priests' and 'clergy' were not quite co-terminous. Where, for instance, did nuns fit in, or Christian Brothers – or, for that matter, Protestant ministers whose role was not nearly as clear as their status?

For I'm afraid, in the heel of the hunt, status, class, caste, was and is what it's all about. And even today, perhaps especially today, it's very hard to convince people that in saying this you're not trying to subvert the idea of an ordained ministry. Of course, priesthood has always and everywhere constituted a class, usually a highly privileged one. The snag is that while Christians have, in history, been no exception to this rule, they *should* be! The systematic clericalisation of Orders seems to have derived mainly from the Church's close involvement with the Roman Empire, east and west, since the

16

fourth century: but the trend was already there, as were the models – both Jewish and Graeco-Roman.

A matter of status. And for a very long time now, a matter of *legal* status. The Code of Canon Law itself makes this explicit: 'By divine institution, among Christ's faithful there are in the Church sacred ministers, who *in law* (my italics) are also called clerics . . . (Can 207). No wonder then that clergy and ministry seem inseparable . . . Oh! and by the way, the Canon goes on to say '. . . the others are called lay people'.

So now we know. We are the 'others', *an fuíoll*. Like the blacks in South Africa? Or all those who, in other times, were neither nobility nor gentry (nor respectable tradesmen). The people in fact. The common people.

And that of course is what we are, and – as they used to say – proud of it! God's people . . . Pobal, populus, 'am, *laos* – and hence laity. But that should mean all of us, including the ordained. The priesthood of the laity is a great and noble doctrine, but I would suggest that equally important is the layhood of the priest, that membership of the *laos* of which his baptism is the sign and guarantee.

I know that I am beginning to repeat myself, but I am convinced that the point has to be made over and over again. The present position has no theological foundation, merely legal sanction: and while law is a great and formidable thing, the Church's law must be rooted in, and be consonant with, the Church's faith and teaching, and with the gospels which are its title deeds. I personally find it hard to see that putting the ordained into a class apart from, over against, and superior to the *laos,* the people as a whole, is so consonant. It rather seems to belong to that 'Gentile' way of doing things which Jesus specifically warned the disciples against (*Mk 10: 42-45*). One might well regard it as the first 'secularising' of the Church!

Partnership
Partnership, you will recall, was one of the things the Cardinal and Bishop Daly said they would be stressing at the Synod, and in fact it's one of the subjects touched on in their joint statement. What a pity that the whole Synod wasn't based on this idea: an exploration of the potential of partnership between the ordained and unordained within the great universal 'laity' which is the People of God. It would have been infinitely preferable to the fervid search for, and expatia-

tion on, 'special' lay elements in mission and ministry and spirituality, as well as 'distinctive' roles and states of life.

I am not indeed suggesting that there is nothing to be said about the mission and ministry of the unordained: there certainly is, and this has to be a main task of the Synod. But it's something to be worked out in the existential situations of the Church throughout the world today, rather than be derived from a 'theology of the laity'. There can be no theology of the laity that is not a theology of the whole Church.

I have already quoted from paragraphs (21,68) of the *Instrumentum Laboris* which specify 'laity' in contexts which clearly apply to all Christians. The point becomes absurdly obvious in statements like:

The laity bring to the world the faith, hope and charity of the Church (par 20)

or

. . . the laity are to strive to overcome the pernicious separation between professed faith and daily life . . . (par 28).

Only the laity? If I were a cleric I'd be insulted by the first of these remarks, and rather puzzled by the second.

Throughout the document there is an emphasis on the 'secular character of the laity' which allows them to accomplish 'in a special way' the salvific mission of the Church in the world, bearing witness to their belonging to Christ, while dealing with temporal things (par 28). This is in itself to be welcomed as reflecting the Church's new 'self-awareness of her mystery and mission in the world' (par 12) – and as paragraph 31, recalling the special place of the laity in the world, remarks: 'If respect for their secular character is kept in mind, the grave danger of *clericalising* the laity will be diminished' (my italics).

Well, I for one have no desire to be clericalised and I can't off-hand remember any layman or woman who does. Nor do I see any 'grave danger' of this happening. Mind you, it's not the first time I've been blind to dangers threateningly visible to my betters (political as well as ecclesiastical). The opposite danger, in this instance, is, we are told, 'marginalisation' – and this does make sense, though more as experience than threat – an old unhappy experience summed up in Talbot's notorious question: 'Who are the laity?'

Encroachment?

Those days are gone, we hope for ever. The laity are clearly there and won't go away, nor indeed does anyone suggest they should. But I have to say that talk of 'clericalisation', especially as something counter to the 'laity's mission in the world', makes me somewhat uneasy. I suspect that some at least who write or speak in these terms are using a kind of code to express concern, anxiety, annoyance at what is seen as encroachment by lay people on the ministry of the ordained, and a consequent devaluing of that ministry. Sometimes the code uses less subtle terms, such as 'sacristy laymen'.

These concerns and attitudes are by no means confined to Ireland, any more than those lay statements and developments which apparently have come to engender them. But I gather that, as far as this country is concerned, what was said and done at the *Pobal* Conference – or, rather, what was *perceived* to be said and done there – has triggered off unmistakable reactions in certain quarters. The suggestion appears to be that these 'unrepresentative' but noisy laity, instead of getting on with their real job in the home, the 'workplace' – the big world in general – want to play at being clergy and running the Church.

I am certain that an unbiased reading of the *Pobal* statements, as published, will show how ludicrously far from the truth this is. But it is true that what emerged loud and clear from the deliberations of the conference working-groups (on which the statements were based) is that these lay people want to *be* the Church in their world, fully and consciously, making use of whatever gifts they have been given to exercise their various ministries in the light of the Spirit. As a corollary of this, they insist that they should be involved in parish and diocesan decision-making, and they go on to say that 'through this involvement, the desirable partnership between the laity, the ordained ministers and the bishops can be made practical reality.' No, they don't want to 'run the Church', but to have a part in it. Again, on the question of worship, they have this to say:

Aware that we have the right and duty because of our baptism to participate fully in public worship, many of us lay people feel angry and frustrated that, twenty years on, Vatican II's vision of active participation by all in a renewed liturgy is still far from full realisation. The gifts which lay people can bring to a liturgical celebration are under-valued and under-used . . .

The paragraph ends: 'There must be a full and equal role for women.' Elsewhere it is stated that 'within the Church women have been patronised and excluded from the decision-making process. This results in their experience of being devalued.' And again, very cogently, 'The Church is impoverished when women are denied equality and their gifts are stifled.' (It was good to hear from Bishop Daly that he has ruled in his own diocese that all commissions and committees must be at least fifty *per cent* composed of women. And the Cardinal has made similar arrangements in Armagh.)

Now, does any or all of this add up to a threat to the ordained? Clearly not, and perhaps the tables could be turned on myself as the one who sees shadows where no realities exist. Indeed I wish this were true. But I cannot purge my perception of the emphasis on the laity's 'mission in the world', and the stated concern over 'clericalisation'. And it gives me no pleasure to say that what I hear coming through is something like 'You people look after the world – leave the Church to us.'

Again, I hope I'm wrong. Even if I'm right, I'm far from attributing unworthy motives to those whose concern is real, though I would hold mistaken. I regard the opposing of Church to world as being as wrong-headed as that of lay to clerical. We are *all* the *laos*, and surely we are all in the world. If not, where are we?

What is the Synod?

On the evidence of the last few pages I hope I won't be accused of writing a 'Begrudger's Guide to the Synod'. It's not what I set out to do. But I think it is only right to point out that expectations are not high. It's certainly a good thing that they shouldn't be *too* high: an exaggerated view of what the Synod might or could do, can be of more harm than good. We have had this in the past, notably in the early days of the institution, when some starry-eyed enthusiasts saw it changing the face of the Church overnight. In fact, while its potential is real, so are its limitations. It is not, repeat *not*, a mini-Council. To quote the useful documentation which Jim Cantwell gave us at the news conference:

> The World Synod of Bishops is a permanent, consultative canonical body which meets at the invitation of the Pope to advise him on matters relating to the teaching, structure, mission or discipline of the Catholic Church.

Representative?

There are other limitations, which are structurally pretty well inevitable: I'm thinking of the 'representative' character of membership. Whatever system is decided upon cannot please everyone, although this one seems to me a reasonable compromise between a strictly mathematical allocation of 'seats' on a population basis and a simple 'one country (or conference) one vote' system: thus Ireland has two representatives as against four from the United States, out of a grand total of 231 bishops. There are special arrangements for the eastern (uniate) churches and the religious orders, and, as well as heads of Curial 'departments', there are thirty Papal nominees (including representatives of *Opus Dei* and *Communione e Liberazione*) – the Pope is, in fact, President of the Synod. The 'Relator-General' (or Moderator) is the Archbishop of Dakar, Cardinal Thiandoum, and there are three 'special secretaries': the Coadjutor Archbishop of Bordeaux and two lay people – one a Portuguese lady who works with the Pontifical Council for the Laity in Rome, and the other a Frenchman who lives in London and is, of all things, head of the Channel Tunnel Consortium . . . I can anticipate a plethora of jokes about the light of the approaching train!

Otherwise, direct lay participation seems to be confined to the sixty auditors of whom we have already heard. Drawn from forty-three countries, they are described as 'nominated by the Pope'. They include Patrick Fay of the Legion of Mary (as noted above); from England, Ms Patricia Jones, a theologian working in Liverpool; Sr Helen McLaughlin, Mother General of the Sacred Heart Order, a Scotswoman living in Rome. Her name, and that of another Sister from America who teaches theology in Los Angeles, remind me once again of Canon 207 which defines the legal status of clerics and lay people. It goes on to say that religious men and women are 'drawn from both groups' – in other words ordained religious are clerics, the rest are lay men and women. The implications of this are interesting: I wonder will there be much discussion on the point at the Synod. It has been give a certain topicality by recent developments in the Franciscan Order (Friars Minor).

A couple of years ago, the Friars (at their General Chapter) approved a proposal 'that the Order be defined as neither clerical nor lay'. This would have made it possible for non-ordained members to be freely elected or appointed to major office in the Order. The proposal was vetoed by the relevant Vatican authority, apparently on the grounds that canon law classifies religious institutes as *either* clerical or lay. As against this, the Minister General of the Order, Fr. John Vaughn (who will be at the Synod) is on record as saying that, while bound to respect the Vatican's decision, 'we know that by its nature the religious life is *neither* clerical nor lay.'

Onwards to Rome!

I am as yet uninformed on the details of the Synod schedule, beyond the first couple of days, which will include an Opening Liturgy (at which the Pope, no doubt, will preside) and a first *Relatio,* to be presented by the Moderator, a working paper on which discussion can be based. A series of plenary sessions will presumably follow.

If the Synod follows established precedent, the participants will at some stage break up into *circuli minores* – working groups representing the principal world languages. As in most such assemblies, these smaller discussion-units usually facilitate closer and more practical examination of issues, leading to more or less concrete proposals, which are then given an airing in the wider forum.

As to what the end product may be, it is at this stage almost impossible to say. We can't even be sure that there will be a statement ready for issue by the end of the proceedings, particularly since 'the function of the Synod is to advise the Pope', not to make decisions. But one would expect a document of some substance to be promulgated at a fairly early date.

In the long run, what we are on about is what I like to think of as the Plain People of God, whose plainness is transformed and transcended by that *communio* of love to which we have been called. To quote Denis Carroll:

> The idea of *communion* is vital. Communion is about relationship and sharing: in love, loyalty, equality, participation. It is about service and compassion. It is about treating each other with respect and justice. It means toleration of difference. It implies trust and confidence. It is the opposite of exclusion because of rank or sex or social condition. It roots in the Eucharistic communion and derives its life from the presence to us of the living Christ in his blessed Spirit . . .

Will the Synod in the thirty days of proceedings bring this message to life for us all? Well, as Ivan Illich said when asked about the after-life: 'I should hope to be surprised.'

The Diary

Thursday 1st October

This morning Pope John Paul was the principal celebrant at the opening Liturgy of the Synod, along with '158 bishops, 38 cardinals, 4 patriarchs and 56 priests'. As to the rest of us, there were I suppose some few hundred in the congregation, but St Peter's was by no means full. I had forgotten how dreadful Roman traffic can be in the morning and so I arrived late at the Basilica but I'd no difficulty in getting a seat. They were singing the *Credo* when I entered so I missed the Pope's homily. However, copies were available at the Sala Stampa, the Vatican Press Office – scene of many a skirmish over the past twenty-five years as the Church painfully learned how to communicate, and the media, equally painfully, tried to learn the Vatican's language (and I don't mean Latin!). There is still no Press Gallery in the Synod Hall, though groups of journalists will be admitted briefly on a 'pool rota'; but the regular bulletins and briefings are now fairly satisfactory.

The Pope spoke this morning in Italian. The English version, from which the following is an extract, was prepared by the Press Office:

> In a few days we shall celebrate the twenty-fifth anniversary of the inauguration of the Second Vatican Council, which dedicated a large part of its Magisterium to our theme. We wish to examine in the light of the experiences of all the churches and communities – the life and mission of the laity in the universal Church.
>
> We wish to examine this question with the eyes of Pastors of the Church, hence from the perspective of our duties and responsibility; from the perspective of our service to the People of God.
>
> In preparing ourselves for it, we have sought to hear from our lay brothers and sisters what they themselves think regarding their life and their mission in the Church.
>
> Some of these lay persons – by necessity a limited number – have been invited to the Synod. It is a matter of a substantial

presence, for the group of lay men and women auditors forms, as it were, the image of the whole laity of the Church. They are mothers and fathers, members of associations, of spiritual movements, of pastoral councils; they are economists, politicians, engineers, educators, catechists; persons belonging to the working world, the world of culture, of industry; persons from both urban and rural settings; they bring to us, together with their witness and their contributions to the discussion, the authentic reality of the commitment of the laity to the mission of the Church for the salvation of the world.

Christ says: 'Whatever you bind on earth shall be bound in heaven, and whatever you loose on earth shall be loosed in heaven' (*Mt 18:18*).

We are confident that the Holy Spirit, who has been given to us in the Church – and for the Church – will help us also to *loose* whatever *needs* to be loosed in this vast sphere of the laity, so that their proper and specific tasks for the ecclesial mission will *spring forth* from their vocation . . .

The Sala Stampa is only a stone's throw from St Peter's, at the top of the Via Della Conciliazione, and as well as providing documents, verbal information, telephone and fax facilities, and desks to work at, it serves as a meeting place, gossip-centre and rumour factory for the print, radio and TV hacks, some resident in Rome but most, like myself, here especially for the Synod. A motley crew if ever there was one, including veterans of Vatican II like Rene Laurentin, Molly Magee, Gary MacEoin and myself, but also bright young men and women on their first outing. We come from all arts and parts but for practical purposes we are divided into five language groups: French, Spanish, English, German and Italian.

We are promised 'a press briefing for each group at approximately 1.00 p.m. whenever a General Assembly is held'. The first assembly didn't take place until five o'clock this evening so we'll have to wait till tomorrow to learn what has happened.

Actually, it appears from the Synod 'Calendar' that the laity theme won't be broached until the third assembly tomorrow evening. This evening and tomorrow morning have been scheduled for the consideration of unfinished business from the previous Synods – including the preparation of a 'Universal Catechism,' a report on the theological status of bishops' conferences, and matters arising from a

Papal document on 'Reconciliation and Penance' following the 1983 Synod.

One item which has trickled out from this evening's assembly is that the Pope made reference to the absence of one of the three Vice-Presidents of the Synod, Cardinal Trinh van Can of Hanoi, and of two other delegate-bishops from Vietnam. It wasn't clear whether they had been refused exit visas or were merely delayed.

Failing more hard information, I regret to say that the main topic of conversation in the Sala was the story, published in several respectable newspapers, of a so far unnamed priest 'somewhere in Italy' who has allegedly had a sex-change. If true, the implications are, to say the least of it, interesting . . .

It was cool (for Rome) when I left to meet friends in Trastevere. They tell me that I have been lucky in avoiding really hot weather, unusually so for September, and consequent *umidita*. Yesterday it was still warm compared to the weather I left behind in Dublin and today has been a pleasant Irish summer's day. I hope it stays that way.

Friday 2nd October

As foreseen yesterday, the Synod has got down to work, but in their first sessions – last evening and this morning – they confined themselves, as predicted, to preliminary matters, mainly relating back to previous Synods. As to the catechism, it appears that a text will not be presented until the next General Synod in 1990; the report of the Study Commission on the Status of Bishops' Conferences will, it is hoped, be circulated before the end of this year. These were the main items discussed last evening, according to a Press Bulletin which we got early this morning: this morning's assembly was the subject of press briefings and a further bulletin before lunch.

Those English-speaking journalists who were here at the last ('Extraordinary') Synod in 1985 were glad to welcome back Monsignor Diarmuid Martin as guide, philosopher and friendly enemy. A brother of Seamus Martin of the *Irish Times,* he is patient, helpful, informative and courteous, with an ability to suffer fools (though, I suspect, not over-gladly). He asked did we want evening briefings also – I and others said 'No!', but our more zealous colleagues out-voted us.

His morning briefing was full and detailed, but as the discussion was on Reconciliation and the Sacrament of Penance, I won't go into it now. Except to note that one or two speakers, when referring to those of the laity who seldom or never go to confession, suggested that this was possibly due to the bad example given them by the clergy!

It was made clear, by the way, that Cardinal Trinh van Can and his fellow bishops have not been allowed to leave Vietnam and will not be at the Synod. The Cardinal's place as Vice-President will be taken by Cardinal Vidal of Cebu. This is sad news, and a very short-sighted move on the part of the Vietnamese authorities.

There are some other absentees, but no indication that they aren't on their way. Cardinal Tomasek of Prague was made especially welcome by the Pope, as representing 'the special Churches which find themselves in great difficulties because of the small number of bishops . . . '

And so, this evening, with preliminaries out of the way, the main theme of the Synod was introduced by the *Relator,* Cardinal Thiandoum. He described his initial report, now to be presented to the fathers, as not intended to supplant the *Instrumentum Laboris* but 'direct our attention towards the Conciliar doctrine: an attempt to focus the problems and render them more specific'. And this is precisely what he did, suggesting four main problem areas, though not the only ones.

1. Secular nature of the vocation and mission of the laity
Further study is necessary of the types of lay activity that can bring about the transformation of the world: motivation, forms of assistance, concrete challenges, formation, norms, etc. The clergy are not excluded from this task so we need to study also mutual relationships within the ecclesial communion. At the same time, liberty of initiative and choice must be ensured. For it is not for the pastors to tell each person what he or she should do, but rather to tell everyone that they should do something. The lay person, for his or her part, should know and appreciate the doctrine of the Church's Magisterium, which lights up his path in what concerns faith and morals. Secularity is not synonymous with secularism.

2. Lay associations and their relationship with pastors

We are experiencing a real blossoming of associations of an evangelical nature – both at international level and within every conceivable grouping of lay persons. At the same time, this growth has not always been harmonious. More careful discernment is being requested, which will give better fruits. Specifically, the presence and weight of the hierarchy in lay associations, a presence which while respecting liberty of action, cannot abdicate its 'pastoral' function, which is proper to those who hold the office of pastors.

3. Secular ministries in the Church today

One of the fruits of the Council was the blossoming of different forms in which the laity could share in the Mission of the Church, a mission which the pastors well know they must share with them. The word 'ministry' was used somewhat carefully in the Council, and exclusively for clerical functions. This is one area in which it is hoped that the Synod will move forward, not merely in so far as terminology is concerned, but also in the preparation to be given, limits, etc. In short, to what point is 'pastoral ministy' the exclusive preserve of pastors?

4. Vocation and mission of the lay woman in the Church and the world

As can be seen in the majority of the replies included in the *Instrumentum Laboris,* there is a total acceptance of the modern movement for the liberation and promotion of women both in the family and in society; equality of rights and responsibilities, etc. But equality does not prevent a recognition of the differences that exist between people. How can a doctrine and way of acting of the Church contribute to this revaluing of equality? While many things which pertain to the sphere of the lay person automatically fall into the masculine and feminine, we must continue to fight against discrimination that is not objective.

Conclusion

These four topics contain some common aspects: formation, cooperation, education in prayer, both liturgical and personal, dialogue . . . even the institutionalised participation in the mission of the Church of the Secular Institutes. It is not the scope of this report to enumerate all the details. It only gives suggestions which may prove a guide to reflection, which itself will discover other lines of thought.

So far so good. 'Reflection' starts tomorrow – No! the five day week has not yet reached the Synod.

Saturday 3rd October

An important lesson I have learned is to always speak of the Church as *we* . . . Together – bishops, priests and lay people – we share responsibility, criticism and praise. We must avoid the language of *us* and *them* when speaking of our different roles in the Church and avoid terms of opposition . . .

Thus Ms Patricia Jones of Liverpool, one of the lay auditors, addressing the Synod this morning on 'Laity and Formation'. The first half of the session was devoted to 'interventions' by five lay speakers who had attended an 'international consultation' in preparation for the Synod, held at Rocca di Papa (some distance from Rome) last May. It was organised by the Pontifical Council for the Laity.

Something over two hundred men and women took part – just like our own *Pobal* gathering. Rather different though in that it was multinational, and that the participants came at the Pope's personal invitation, many of them representing organisations and movements. They met for four days and used the *Instrumentum Laboris* as a guideline for their discussion.

The report to the Synod indicated considerable enthusiasm and commitment, with an emphasis on spirituality, dialogue within the Church and with the world, the mission of women in a variety of social and cultural contexts – this last being also the subject of a further meeting of women only in Brussels in June, which considered 'difficulties' experienced by women 'involved in the Church and in the world . . . precisely because they were women'. And there was great insistence on the word *formation* (a word against which I, personally, react rather negatively – but, no matter!) On this, Patricia Jones made four points:

1. The purpose of formation is to release in people the power which is within them . . . Formation takes place when people respond

to the call of God and live their ordinary lives as the mission given them by Christ. I ask the Synod to affirm ordinary Catholics who in their daily lives seek to live as the heart of the Church in the heart of the world. For this we need an integrated theological vision of the unity of the sacred and the secular.

2. The home and source of formation is the parish. The parish community can reach out and evangelise people whom the lay movements may never touch . . . and can draw people into ministries that are not a flight from the world but a deeper involvement in the life of God in the world.

3. Patterns of collaborative ministry encourage the realisation and employment of all the gifts given by God to his people. There should be no unemployment in the Church. Particular recognition should be given to the vocation of lay people in full-time pastoral ministry.

4. Formation must prepare people to play their full part in political life. This is a consequence of baptism. It will bring conflict within ourselves and our communities, but even this is part of our witness to the Cross of Christ . . .

An unexpected note was struck by Ms Chooi of Malaysia when she referred to 'the area of transparency and accountability in all that affects the financial position and activities of the Church at all levels, from the smallest ecclesial community to the international level of the Holy See'. Referring to attacks and allegations made in the media, she said:

We love the Church and want to defend it against unjust attacks. But we need information at our disposal that can allow us to show to the world that we have nothing to hide . . .

And so say all of us!

In the second part of the session, seven of the fathers began their reflections on the theme – as outlined by the *Relator*, and elsewhere.

Cardinal Sin of Manila made an interesting point when he said that politics and religion were inseparable in Asia – unlike the west. He should know . . . Bishop Aubry of La Reunion issued a timely reminder that 'there is not the Church on one side and the world on another'. Cardinal Daneels of Brussels insisted that 'women should first and foremost fulfil the place that is due them in the administration of the diocese' and that they 'must not lose sight of the irreplaceable role of women religious.'

'The near total silence' of the *Instrumentum Laboris* on the situation of young people was criticised by Archbishop Pimenta of Bombay. He spoke of youth today as 'a youth in ferment, and in some cases . . . living in fear because of an uncertain future. On the other hand, a vast majority . . . is finding religion irrelevant to their lives . . . and for many, whether God exists or not has ceased to be an issue . . . ' He asked the Synod to take a fresh look at Confirmation, 'the sacrament of Christian adulthood', and at ministries to and for young people.

The final speaker this morning was Bishop Gabriel Balet of Mondou in Chad:

> From January 1979 to December 1986, civil war raged in the regions where 90% of Christians live; and in 1986 and 1985 there was, in addition, a drought . . . Thanks to the active faith of the laity, especially in the zones off-limits to foreigners, most of the Christian communities grew in number and in spiritual depth. From this fact, the laity understood better that they were responsible no longer before priests or religious women (foreigners for the most part), but before their own community . . .

Happy declericalisation! That sort of witness makes some of our own concerns rather trivial.

No assembly this evening. The Pope and the fathers are taking part in a Vigil of Prayer in St Peter's with several lay groups.

Sunday 4th October

This is the Feast of St Francis. I always think that the quality of the Italian people is reflected in their choice of Francis as their patron. This evening, the Mayor of Rome will make the traditional presentation of a 'votive chalice' to the Provincial of the Friars Minor in Ara Coeli – not the house where Cardinal Ó Fiaich lives in Armagh, but the ancient church on the Campodoglio where the Friars have their headquarters.

Of course, Franciscan links between Ireland and Italy have been strong for centuries; the first of the *bráithre* arrived not long after the founder's death. And since the seventeenth century the church and college of St Isodore on the Via degli Artisti – just behind the Via Veneto – has belonged to the Irish. Today it bears on its gate the inscription *Coláiste Proinsiasach Gaelach*. An old *pietas* brought me to Mass there this morning; the Guardian, David O'Reilly, was most hospitable, but the celebrant was another Francis, a younger member of the community, keeping his *onomastico*, his 'name day' – much more important here than a birthday. The liturgy and the homily were well worth the journey, though I was sad at the absence of *Gaeilge*. Shades of Aodh Mac Aingil!

Ironically, as more than one member of the congregation told me over coffee, Mass in English is what first brought them there, and they are now regulars! I suppose the same applies in San Clemente and St Patrick's, where Irish Dominicans and Augustinians, respectively, are in charge. The latter is called Ireland's 'national' church; it was built in this century and scores of Irish marriages are celebrated there each year. San Clemente I'll have a word to say about another day.

Talking about language, Latin seems to be having a revival at the Synod. It is, of course, in theory, the official language but modern languages 'may' be used and in recent years have been in the majority. This year many Third World fathers have been making their contributions in Latin – several of them with considerable elegance. As an unrepentant vernacularist, I nevertheless welcome the return to favour of Latin where an *international* medium is genuinely required, as it clearly is among 'minority' language groups. (Not that I don't think it has an important liturgical role also – even at home – at least in sung liturgies. Bringing in Irish or English should not mean throwing Latin out the window. It's not a case of either/or . . .)

Going to St Isodore's meant that I was not present at the Beatification Liturgy in St Peter's when the Pope beatified three young lay Europeans of our time, all three of them described as martyrs. One, a Breton worker, died in a Nazi death camp in 1945.

Monday 5th October

The first speaker at this morning's session was Auxiliary Bishop James Robinson of Sydney. I was pleased to hear him describe the term 'laypersons' as rather negative (as compared with 'Christ's faithful' which applies to all), and to deprecate emphasis on 'specifically lay' activities at the expense of 'that rich field of action that is common to all Christ's faithful . . . ' A similar view was expressed by another Auxiliary, Bishop Bullet of Lausanne: 'It is necessary,' he said, 'first to speak of ecclesial communion, of the mission and vocation common to all, before specifying functions proper to each one. *It is necessary to avoid the division: Church-priest/laity-world'*. (Italics mine).

Again, Bishop Karlen of Bulawayo in Zimbabwe:

> There is no duality of mission, as if the Church were entrusted to the clergy and the world to the laity . . .

Bishop Shimamoto of Urawa (Japan):

> Lay Christians are not just the bridge between the Church and the world; they are the Church itself present in the world. Their secularity is the Church's secularity . . .

Each of these four speakers expressed what I regard as a very necessary correction to the over-simplified lay-cleric/world-Church dualisms I've already referred to. I hope there'll be more to come.

Other matters raised this morning included the challenge of the disabled – 'one fifth of the world's population' (Fr Boyle, Superior General of the Passionists); the urgent need for 'part-time priests' in several Asian countries (Archbishop Legaspi of Caceres in the Philippines); the 'front-line' position of lay people in inter-faith dialogue, for example in Muslim and Hindu environments (Cardinal Arinze, President of the Secretariat for Non-Christians). And we were reminded by Bishop Porras Cardoso from Venezuela that:

> . . . the vocation and mission of the laity must take as a starting point the reality that surrounds their concrete world. For the Third World countries, plunged in poverty, the call of faith comes through the preferential option for the poor.

Two of those who spoke on women and the Church are, perhaps, worth quoting at some length. First, Archbishop Rembert George Weakland of Milwaukee, who is a Benedictine:

> Co-discipleship in the Church means appreciating the gifts of women and seeing new ways in which they can contribute fully to Church life and leadership. Women ask to be treated in a mutual relationship that is not condescending or paternalistic, that does not create passivity or dependency. Women wish to be treated in the way Jesus treated women; with trust and respect. Non-ordination to priesthood must not be seen as a manifestation of baptismal inferiority.

The Church must also struggle to root out any sexism in society where women can so often be treated as inferior, especially in wages or advancement, or as objects.

Practical steps that could be taken at once include the permitting of all liturgical roles that do not require ordination to women and men, the opening to all laity of decision-making and administrative roles on the diocesan level and on the level of the Roman Curia and diplomatic corps, the use of language in liturgy and official documents that include women, the fostering of collaborative models of work between clergy and laity that are not based on inferiority and dependency, and the supporting of family values and the role of women in home and society.

Equally strong was Bishop Gerhard Schwenzer of Oslo:

The Church defends in her documents the dignity and rights of women. Although Vatican Council II clearly recognised the fundamental equality between men and women, we must state that, twenty years after the Council, there exists still in many women a widespread feeling of powerlessness and disappointment.

Independent of the fact of whether this feeling exists rightly or mistakenly, we must take it seriously and take consequent action. Is the reality according to which men and women are equal actually recognised in practice? This reality presupposes a sensitising from the interior of priests; that is to say the method and manner in which women are 'seen' in general, how they are treated, addressed and spoken of.

Educated women, whose positive attitude within the Church is recognised, ought to have many other positions of responsibility in comparison to those they've held until now in the pastoral area (for example, collaboration in workshops) in the Church community, up to the Curia. It is important that women themselves be able to give their contribution to the necessary changes.

The insufficient entry of women into the ecclesiastical environment is being experienced ever more as a fundamental failure of the Church. In no case are women only the *object* of pastoral ministry but rather *subjects* responsible, in great measure and indispensably, in the life of the Church, and therefore as much in the spread of the faith as in the participation in pastoral ministry and *diaconia*. This awareness must be strengthened internally in the Church at every level and must be transformed into concrete action.

I suppose that when most of us in Ireland think of the Church in the Third World, Latin America and the Philippines are what come most readily to mind. This is understandable, but it's good to be reminded of the realities of Africa and Asia in all their complex variety. This has been happening at the Synod; on Saturday I quoted a bishop from Chad who spoke of a Church, starved of priests, surviving and indeed flowering in adversity. This evening we heard from the Bishop of Nakuru in Kenya who spoke of the 'tangible hope of the African Christian for a greater involvement of the laity in the life of the Church in the third millenium. Theirs is a founded hope . . . fruit of a new vision of Vatican II's ecclesiology which envisions the Church as "The New People of God".' As witness to this new hope he pointed to his people's 'joyful enthusiasm and commitment at liturgical celebrations, and in the life of our small christian communities. The laity are no longer mere spectators.' And he ended: 'A new impetus is rightly expected of the Synod . . . call it a Pentecostal Echo of Vatican II.'

Another African reality came to us in the intervention of Archbishop Rafael Nze Abuy of Malabo, Equatorial Guinea:

> From the very beginning of the activity of the missionaries, who brought the Gospel and Catholicity to our young churches, the essential figure of the lay catechist emerged. The presence of these laymen was decisive in the implanting of the Church in our land; and continues to be so in this period of maturing of the faith and inculturation. During the prolonged absence of the missionaries, it was they who nurtured the faith in more distant villages. Because of their knowledge of the customs of their people and their blood brothers, they were and continue to be very often, the intermediaries between the missionaries and the people, like incarnated interpreters of the Gospel message in the midst of their neighbours.
>
> Our present task is to define what they can and should be doing in the future, in our local churches and in our society, as committed Catholics.

Of course, some things are common to north and south, among rich and poor. Bishop Rovalo Azcue from Mexico sounded a familiar call when he said:

> It is extremely important to speak in this Synod about the presence of the young lay person in the Church . . . In Mexico,

for example, there were in 1985, seventeen million young people between the ages of 15 and 24. By 1990, there will be twenty million, 22.8% of the population. The same applies in many other countries . . . A Church that is seeking to make the Second Vatican Council a reality needs her young laity . . .

An important pastoral problem is to find a way of bringing the person of Jesus to the many young people who don't go to Church or take part in group meetings . . . It is urgent to go out into the streets and announce the Gospel there . . .

Once again the question of women was raised, this time by Bishop Russell Saines of Hamilton in New Zealand. He made a special plea on behalf of 'single women, solo mothers and divorced women (who) feel they are alienated from the Church'.

Finally, and returning to fundamentals, Bishop Patrick D'Souza of Varanasi in India:

The theme of the Synod can be approached from two different perspectives. One would consist in starting from the distinction between clergy and laity as it has evolved over the centuries. Such an approach would stress the differences, study the laity largely in contrast to the priestly ministry, and assign it to the 'Consecrato Mundi' as its specific competence in contrast to the sacred sphere belonging to the clergy. This perspective, however, appears narrow.

The other perspective, solidly founded in the concept of the Church as *communio* would emphasise the fundamental priestly reality based on the baptismal consecration, which is common to all the members of the People of God. It would insist on the one common mission of the Church, shared by all her members, through a variety of charisms, functions and ministries, and would foster participatory leadership at all levels. It would surpass the narrow dichotomies which do not correspond to the reality, such as clergy-laity, sacred-secular, spiritual-temporal, church-world. The Church is not opposed to the world; it is in, of and for the world. And so also are all services and ministries inter-related and inter-dependent.

A fair day's work!

Tuesday 6th October

The Synod fathers are certainly kept busy. In this phase of the proceedings, which continues for another week, there are two plenary sessions, Monday till Friday, with a Saturday morning session, and other weekend activities planned. The normal timetable is 9.00am to 12.30pm and again 5.00pm to 7.00pm (which in practice means, as Cardinal Ó Fiaich told me the other evening, at a dinner he hosted for Irish reporters, they have to be up for Mass at 7.00am).

It's all necessary, I suppose, to give everyone a chance to be heard. This morning, for example, twenty of the 216 bishops present spoke; this evening a mere thirteen. I expect that the two Irish voices may be heard on tomorrow and Thursday. (There is, of course, a third Irishman present, Patrick Fay, but I have no indication that he will be given an opportunity to speak.)

It's still far too early to see or say 'how the Synod is going' — although there are certain hopeful indications. There's a great variety of opinions and points of view being expressed. So, today I thought it might be a good idea to give the flavour of all this in a series of brief quotes — a sort of 'Today they said'. Thus:

How to avoid the laity's remaining at an almost infantile level in the Church? . . .By creating wider channels of participation (with the possibility of reaching *ecclesiastical responsibility* . . .)
Archbishop Diaz Merchan of Oviedo

The harsh Asian reality of poverty and misery reminds us that 'Asia groans with pain, like the pain of childbirth' (*Rom 8:22*). Deep in the heart of Asia the Paschal Mystery of Jesus is being remembered and relived. These realities force on us the urgency of the need to mobilise all the People of God in an atmosphere of communion, collegiality and co-responsibility . . .
Archbishop Henry D'Souza of Calcutta

The Christian lay person is not someone who is lacking something, but rather an integral member of the Body of Christ.
Cardinal Wetter, Archbishop of Munich & Freising

If the grace of baptism takes precedence over all distinctions of responsibility or office, then it is the assembly of baptised persons which is the first subject of ministry.

It is the foremost bearer of the Word, the foremost agent of reconciliation, the foremost builder of communion.

Archbishop Chiasson of Moncton, Canada

The apostolate demands not only interior formation but courage as well: the contemporary world is marked by cowardice and fear! And it is precisely upon these human weaknesses that dictatorships build their dominions . . . Lord, you call me — here I am! I am ready!

Cardinal Tomasek, Archbishop of Prague

History tells us that, in former times, certain civil leaders used to receive the diaconate — and also that the laity were consulted when bishops were being elected. It reminds us that married men and fathers of families may still possibly be ordained priests . . .

Patriarch Sfeir, Maronite Patriarch of Antioch

It is pleasant to report that the laity in Tanzania . . . find no time to fight their way into the sacristy, either to seek employment or to express their Catholic identity. They are happy to find the time for the evangelisation of politics, economy and society.

Archbishop Pengo of Tunduru—Masasi

In countries where Catholics are deprived of the right to create their own associations, the Church must remind all that this is not a privilege, but a right rooted in the natural law.

Cardinal Macharski, Archbishop of Cracow

In basic christian communities . . . the historical dimension of the Kingdom of God is verified in the midst of actions that scandalously oppose the building of that Kingdom: inhuman pay-structures, unemployment, drug traffic, indifference to need, administrative corruption.

Bishop Terrazas Sandoval CSSR of Oruro, Bolivia

We hope that in accentuating the secular nature of the laity we will not be making divisions in the service of God and of the world, and a distinction between clergy and laity. The service of God and the world is a single reality . . . We are grateful for some 150 years of existence of Catholic organisations. The result of the free initiative of lay persons, they provide a forum where Church and world can meet.

Bishop Hemmerle of Aachen on behalf of the German Episcopal Conference

Among women there is a group that merits special mention: the single woman, one who by God's design and her own decision has adopted the single state. By reason of their number, their presence in all environments, and their maturity, they signify an extraordinary force for the spread of the Gospel.

Bishop Munoz Nunez of Aguascalientes, Mexico

The Church in South Africa . . . is caught in the crossfire between oppressor and liberator, between one ideology of liberation and another. Criticising one side, she finds herself exploited by another; expressing concern for all, she satisfies none . . . She has to find a concrete methodology – through a process of pastoral planning – by which she can be present at the heart of political change, in a way that fits with her own identity and mission.

Bishop Napier, OFM, of Kokstad

As I've said, there were a total of thirty-three speakers today, so the bit I've quoted represents less than half of what was said. There were two interventions I should like to note more fully. The first (because of who and what he is) by Cardinal Joseph Ratzinger, Prefect of the Congregation for the Doctrine of the Faith:

My contribution will try to clarify the concept of 'lay', distinguishing four levels of meaning. In the theological-classical concept which distinguishes the 'cleric' and the 'layperson' it is necessary to observe that the priest is a concept of relationship: 'For you I am bishop, with you I am Christian' (Augustine). The priest is essentially defined in comparison to the community through his relationship with Christ; the lay person, on the other hand, does not find his definition in relationship with the priest, but in a series of further relationships.

The second level of meaning is of a sociological-functional nature. Whoever assumes a fulltime permanent function within the Church is not *in this sense* a lay person: his specific problems in reference to the Church cannot in any case be presented as problems of the laity.

The third level of meaning regards models of spiritual life. St Francis de Sales pointed out that there is no absolutely uniform spirituality of Christians or of the laity, but rather many diverse forms.

From this viewpoint, no one is simply and only a lay person. Today the many and different spiritualities find particular expression in various spiritual movements, in which the insertion of the laity in the Church is concretely realised.

The fourth level of meaning is historical and eschatological: the Church must not become the world, nor the world the Church; but all Christians must prepare the Church and the world for the coming of the Kingdom of God.

In considerable contrast to Cardinal Ratzinger's statement, we have a voice from one of the ancient churches of the East: Bishop Kunnasserry of the Syro-Malabar church in India, which, he said, traditionally focused 'on the holy people of God, gathered around the Risen Lord'. He developed this idea:

So the *laos* or laity came in the first place and the hierarchy and the clergy were rightly considered the leaders and ministers called to serve the people . . . It felt itself as the grace-acting community, with every member having a share in the sanctifying role of the Church.

There was a wide involvement of the whole Church, both men and women, in the celebration of the sacraments: this is particularly evident in the role of the *Msamsanitha* or deaconess who was especially ordained to help in the administration of baptism to women, to distribute Holy Communion under special circumstances and form, etc. Even today the ordination service of bishops in Oriental Rites contains words explicitly conferring power to ordain deaconesses. It will be opportune to restore the institution of deaconess, in the present day context.

The Eucharist was the communitarian service of the whole people. It began with the celebration of the Word in the middle of the Church, the people standing around the bishop and the clergy. Then their gifts moved to the eastern end of the church where the altar was located. All through, the Divine Liturgy appeared a celebration of the people led by the bishop . . . There was an intimate relationship between the people and their priests. No one could be accepted for priestly training or ordained without the consent of the *palliyogam* or parish council. Priestly formation was not merely a training for ministry but an ongoing interaction between the people and those selected to lead them . . . Sacred functions, including the Divine Liturgy, began with the celebrant formally asking the permission of the people.

Did I hear someone whisper 'Sacristy Laity'?

Wednesday 7th October

This evening has been listed as the second occasion on which the Synod is to hear from the auditors. They have, by the way, been the subject of some comment in the Sala Stampa, as it was alleged that they have been 'forbidden to talk to the media'. When asked about it, Diarmuid Martin, who is invariably as good-humoured and reassuring as Brian Lenihan*, 'explained' that they were simply bound by the normal Synod rules.

Diligent perusal of the Synod 'Order' (amended edition 1975) casts little light on this. But yesterday we were told that the General Secretary, Jan Schotte, reminded the fathers that, in principle, everything was confidential except what was released. A Vatican solution to a Vatican problem, which leaves us back at square X. On the practical level, of course, Diarmuid and his colleagues continue to serve.

Two things, however, need to be said. One: although the briefings are remarkably good, given the time available to prepare them, and the Press Office summaries are usually prepared by the speakers themselves, it's hard to see why, generally speaking, full texts are not available – *if the speakers are willing to release them*. This last provision would meet the only argument that made sense in that we heard of the General Secretary's *apologia*: that bishops from certain countries would not wish everything they say to be reported to, and probably used against them by, hostile regimes.

Two: Peter Hebblethwaite (old Vatican hand, author of a splendid biography of John XXIII and now engaged in another of Paul VI, European correspondent of the American *National Catholic Reporter*) said the other day that it's quite ridiculous that responsible media reporters are not admitted to the Synod Hall, as they are to assemblies on the highest level all over the world. (I've referred to this already and I agree entirely with Hebblethwaite.) Are they not to be trusted to report accurately and honestly? It's a professional in-sult, reminiscent, to an Irishman, of the notorious order issued under Section 31 of the Broadcasting Act.

Further developments in the Vietnam story. According to the General Secretary, who read a statement at the beginning of this morning's session, Cardinal Trinh Van Can's absence is due to his

---

*Brian Lenihan, Minister for Foreign Affairs, Haughey Government 1987 –. Favourite phrase: 'No problem!'

weak physical condition – the phrase used in the Cardinal's own telegram of apology (sent on September 20!), in which he said that the other two Vietnamese bishops would be coming. They haven't yet arrived. Curiouser and curiouser!

Also absent are two from Czechoslovakia who were invited by the Pope: Monsignor Jan Hirka and a lay auditor, Mr Silvester Krcmery. So far they have not been allowed to come, although at the end of September the General Secretary asked the Czech Prime Minister to intervene.

Whatever happened *glasnost?*

☆

One third of this morning's interventions were by bishops from black Africa, dwelling, naturally enough, on their own special problems, although not all of these were new to the rest of us. Thus the Bishop of Banjul in the Gambia (who bears the good Gambian name of Michael J. Cleary!):

> Some laity report that, after they have attended seminars, retreats and animation courses geared to producing committed and responsible laity, they are not allowed, by some priests and religious, to participate in the work in the way they have been encouraged . . .

The Auxiliary Bishop of Cochabamba in Bolivia spoke quietly of '. . . marginalisation and exploitation of the majority of our people. This *forces* us to revise the model of the Church . . . and decide for the Church – People of God, reaffirming her option for the poor . . . and the building of the Kingdom of God *here and now.'*

'Exploitation' was a word used also by Bishop Guevarra of Balanga in the Philippines as he spoke of 'the plight of Asian women':

> In Asia, tourism and the entertainment industries have exploited, degraded and dehumanised Asian women . . . In general, Asian society views women as inferior . . . (though) in some countries their advancement is phenomenal. Their work in the Church is extremely valuable: without them, evangelisation would collapse.
>
> The principles of dignity and equality are equally applicable *within* the Church. It is only thus that the Church will be credible when she speaks with a voice that has no equal in Asia . . . '

41

In the same spirit, Cardinal Decourtray, Archbishop of Lyon, said:
It is true that many women are at ease in the Church; it is also a fact that many feel themselves victims of a lack of objective *respect* on the part of pastors.

He wanted the Synod to encourage theological study into the *meaning of femininity* in God's design and to determine some 'typical responsibilities' to which women might be called, e.g. spiritual counsel (as in eastern monastic tradition), formation of Christians and especially of priests.

The Superior General of the Society of the Divine Word, Fr Heinrich Heekeren, emphasised the need for a sound biblical basis for lay activity, because 'ignorance of the scriptures is ignorance of Christ'. An active lay Ministry of the Word would, inter alia, 'shorten the distance which still separates us from the other Churches' and curtail 'the alarming inroads being made by the aggressive anti-ecumenical approach of certain sects.'

Following the teachings of Paul VI and the present Pope, the Bishop of Przemysl (Poland) spoke of the need to create: 'the primacy of persons over things; the primacy of ethics over technology; the primacy of being over having; the primacy of charity over justice . . . '

☆

'The presence of the laity in the world' was the subject addressed by the seven auditors who spoke in this evening's session. These were: Ms Mavis Pirola from Australia – she and her husband Ron represent Marriage Encounter; Etienne Bisimwa from Zaire, who is Secretary General of the International Catholic Student Movement; Enrique Marius, a trade unionist from Venezuela; Ms Albina Aspell, President of the National Catholic Press Association, USA and Canada; Ms Antoinette Prudence, President of the International Movement of the Apostolate of Children, from Rodriguez in the Indian Ocean; Nicholas Lobkowicz and Salvatore Nocera, neither of whom is on the list of auditors, and neither of whom is known to the omniscient Diarmuid.

Ms Pirola spoke on 'The Family and the Mission of the Laity'. Pointing out that the family is the basic Christian community, where the vast majority receive their 'formation', she insisted that marriage and family life should enrich all aspects of the laity's mission and not be seen as a separate 'issue'. Three of her points were particularly striking.

First:

> Sexual intimacy is what distinguishes matrimony from all other Christian relationships. The sexual nature of this sacrament needs to be affirmed, for the sake of the couples, their families and the whole Church. An appreciation of the value of their sexual intimacy will be important in fostering a better understanding of the Church's teaching on the transmission of life.

Second:

> The large increase in the numbers of single parent families in recent years has drawn attention to their special needs. However, they are also a resource in the Church's mission. They participate in Christ's redemptive mission in a special way. Furthermore they bring special qualities of their own to the rest of the community, such as courage in adversity, adaptability to change, and constancy of faith in the face of lost hopes and dreams.

And third:

> It is also important to develop the concept of mission *by* families as well as *to* them. By virtue of their position in the neighbourhood, and their flexibility and relatability, they are a powerful evangelising influence. The hospitality of the home is especially important in this regard. Towards this end, a family perspective in the formation of priests is important. Our hope is that this Synod on the Laity will uncover and utilise the resources of the family for the sake of the Kingdom.

Etienne Bisimwa spoke movingly of 'the cries and anguish of millions of young people who live in poverty and who are trapped in a life without a future'. In their resistance to the movements that marginalise them there are signs of religious awakening, but also of a decline towards secularism and 'the practical atheism of life'. How to communicate the Good News today? It is essential that the Church *listen* to the concrete situations of the young. There is a thirst for the

Word of God among them, as well as a real thirst for a theological formation that will deepen their faith.

Enrique Marius, on the 'World of Work', was forthright in what he had to say:

> The hopes that workers placed in this Synod are many: therefore it causes some surprise and reflection that in the *Instrumentum Laboris* there are only 22 lines of reference to the working world.
>
> By looking at the world of work and at the man who works or who aspires to work, that is to say, the great majority of humanity, we can state that human life is making us each day less human.
>
> It is our responsibility to transmit the anxieties and the hopes of many millions of workers, especially in the so-called Third World, who, even by working in humiliating conditions more than ten hours daily, no longer are able to respond to the basic necessities of themselves and their families; who are humiliated each time they demand the possibility of work; who lose hope when they are discriminated against in work or in social or political life.
>
> There must be a primacy of work over capital and technology, to assume it as a primary cause of development, to project it as a fundamental factor of 'culturisation', to recentre it in those actions as an inherent element in the proper dignification of man.
>
> The commitment of the Christian also involves the restructuring of workers' organisations, in order to overcome the dependence on domineering leadership-centres of international power, to guarantee the full participation of all workers, to develop solidarity as an essential value.
>
> But the fundamental thing is to make human life more human, moving towards the integral liberation of workers and peoples, fully assuming the cultural identity which flows from work and service to men. They are steps of immediate urgency for the humanisation of society and the building of the Culture of Love.

Ms Aspell, on 'The World of the Mass Media', said that:
> A free flow of information has the power to avert problems, stop rumour and erase suspicion . . . To mature, intelligent Catholics this flow of information is as much the living water of modern faith as the prayer we offer daily. Without it, members of the Church dry up and wither.

Few of us would disagree, even if we wouldn't put it quite like that.

Ms Prudence, speaking of 'The Apostolate of Children', began by pointing out that children's frustration over the 'serious societal problems' which many of them face today is aggravated by the fact that adults 'often neglect to elicit their opinion or their contribution'. But she also said that, across the world, children are 'not giving in to passivity' and are doing many things to change the course of events and carry the Good News into the realities of life: Mr Lobkowiz's remarks on 'Culture and the mission of the laity' I personally found rather obscure. He seemed to convey the impression that culture could and should be 'changed' and 'corrected'. This complex task offered a challenge to 'students and young intellectuals seeking answers in their search for a meaning to life'. Actually, I'm not at all sure what Mr Lobkowicz means by culture.

There was nothing obscure about Mr Nocera's intervention, which he wrote in braille and which was read to the Synod on his behalf. His own disability, and his involvement in work with and for other handicapped people in Italy and in the Third Word, gave considerable authority to what he had to say. He affirmed that, while many non-believers have found strength in Christian faith, many believers – because of individual insensitivity and that of civil and ecclesial bodies have 'lost their faith, crushed by pain, living on the fringes of society'.

He deprecated pastoral approaches to the disabled and their families which relied exclusively on the Cross and the value of suffering – without reference to the resurrection – and asked that paragraphs 49 and 72 of the *Instrumentum Laboris* be revised in this context.

Mr Nocera asked the administrators of large special institutes for the handicapped to restructure them in the form of small communities and territorial services of more human dimensions. And he ended: 'Proclaim this message also to the secular world which, considering us 'invalids' according to the logic of consumerism and the ethic of efficiency, wishes to eliminate us through abortion or euthanasia.'

So, we're half-way through the first half, if you follow me. We're due another week of plenary sessions, by the end of which every possible angle of the theme should have been exhaustively dealt with. Or do I mean exhaustingly?

Good night. Sometimes I wonder what's the point of the whole damn thing . . .

Thursday 8th October

When I woke up this morning, after careful consideration and two cups of tea, I decided there *was* some point to what's going on, although I couldn't quite put my finger on it. However I decided that, in this second half of the first half – if, once again, you follow me – while the Fathers continue to roll on like a rushing river, I would only try to halt the flow, and divert it to these pages, if something *new* was being said. But then quite a lot is – more than you'd think.

It was indeed 'new', not to say *news*, to me that the people of Nicaragua 'possess a desire, which they share with their Bishops to evangelise political life, *coupled with a rejection of the politicisation of the Gospel.*' So said the Auxiliary Bishop of Bluefields (Nicaragua). What, I ask myself, can he mean?

The Superior General of the Priests of the Most Blessed Sacrament, Fr Anthony McSweeney (Australia), had something new to say about the Eucharist. Or something so old and true we might have forgotten it.

> Fully-formed Christians show the power of the Sacrament in their lives, but for vast numbers today the Eucharist functions as almost their last contact with the Church. With the atomising of the Christian social body, *Sacraments tend to be treated as consumer products* . . .
>
> A Eucharistic spirituality is needed. Rooted in prayer, it must be fully incarnational, communitarian, ecumenical and social, as well as profoundly personal . . .
>
> As Sacrament of Unity, the Eucharist offers a pattern for an ecclesial style of tolerance and respect . . . ordering every gift and charism to communion.

(The Priests of the Blessed Sacrament are the community who have the chapel in D'Olier Street, Dublin, where the old 'Red Bank' used to be.)

Again, another new/old thought from Bishop Devin of Motherwell:

> The laity are more concerned about their own salvation than the evangelisation of the world . . .

New, only because, I suppose, we haven't been thinking that way, is what Bishop Raobelina from Madagascar said:

> One might say that our country, and developing countries in general, will be able to move out of their under-development effectively and know a more harmonious and equitable evolution only in the measure in which political 'decision-makers' and what one could call 'intermediate decision-makers' . . . technicians, teachers, economists . . . are awakened to a sense of the common good and justice. Such a situation constitutes a challenge for the Church. Could the Synodal Assembly study means for putting into practice concretely a pastoral ministry that is better adapted to persons in responsibility in our societies?

> The Church, in order to be relevant and meaningful to its world of oppression, denial of human rights, etc. must encourage and sustain laity sensitive to the political situation of the place – a laity who see, hear and react as Jesus Christ did to his context.

> Hence, let us cease from *cautioning the laity* not to enter deeply with secularity of social development or politics, but encourage them and evaluate their involvement as *true apostolate* and *true spirituality* and a new form of living in their faith, a new form of discipleship.

New? Certainly in the naked honesty of what the bishop had to say. He must have annoyed at least four different kinds of 'good Catholics'. I'd love to meet him.

And Bishop Rodrigues da Costa of Macau – one of the Pope's special nominees – was certainly new in the way he carried old ideas to their contemporary logical conclusion.

> *Instrumentum Laboris* no. 25 has spoken about the importance of the *Sensus Fidei* of the people of God. If our Synod is to *'go forward'* from what is taught in Vatican II – *Lumen Gentium* no. 12 – we have to find ways and means of consulting the faithful, not only the theologically educated clergy but all the people of

God as much as we can. It means new structures for *listening to them eagerly,* encouraging them to speak fearlessly about their needs, *consulting them on how to realise our projects* in the diocese, in the parish, with regard to liturgy, with regard to social apostolate, with regard to political involvement etc.

We clergy have a communion of life with them. Unless and until we consult and give them a place in our decisions regarding faith and morals, the laity will only belong to the Church and will not become the Church. Let this Synod put an end to the old passive and blindly obedient laity and encourage vigilant, active and collaborative laity in the matter of discerning and living our faith and morals.

Bishop Celso José Pinto da Silva, of Vitoria da Conquista, along with all who have eyes to see and ears to hear in Brazil, has come to terms with a new situation – and done so gladly:

Before the Council the laity who were most committed to apostolic action of the Church in Brazil belonged to the middle and upper class. The poor were considered the object of their pastoral contribution. Now, on the other hand, the presence of the poor is growing, as aware and active Christians, participants in the life and mission of the Church.

This fact is not the fruit of a pre-determined pastoral plan, but of a gradual opening on the part of the Church to the 'cries' of the impoverished and oppressed people of our country. The poor 'have invaded' the Church. They bring with them their aspirations for justice and fraternity along with the hope of faith.

'New' in another sense was Archbishop Angelini's plea that the Synod's final document should give 'proper and deserved attention [to] the health-care apostolate'. Archbishop Angelini is in charge of the new Curial department for the apostolate of health-care workers on all levels – an initiative of Pope John Paul.

There were also a number of speeches on lay 'movements'. But that's another story for another day.

☆

No briefings today. Instead, all the press-gang (including a few who, God knows how, have got accreditation, without ever having, I should say, uttered a published word) – all, whatever our provenance or tribal dialect, were gathered into the main hall of the Sala Stampa for a formal Press Conference.

It was, as these things so often are, something of a non-event. It may have been redeemed for some, afterwards, in personal contact – which again is, after all, par for the course.

Of the four persons on the panel: Ms Chooi, the auditor from Kuala Lumpur; Archbishop Stephen Naidoo of Capetown; Bishop Castrillón Hoyos of Perija in Colombia; and Mr Dherse of the Channel Tunnel – Archbishop Naidoo was the only one who said anything. Most questions were fielded: charmingly by Ms Chooi, boringly by Mr Tunnel, and ponderously by Bishop Castrillón. But the Archbishop was impressive, and he seemed to be genuinely trying to inform. As a member of the Information Committee of the Synod, one might say this is what he was there for, but such considerations don't always count. One thing he promised to look into was the alleged Wall of Secrecy being built between Synod members and the rest of us – a new, unpleasant development, which doesn't seem to be just a figment of fevered journalists. For instance (and for the first time) bishops' and auditors' phone numbers are not being released . . . And, for God's sake, why not? They can be found eventually, so why make more trouble for hard-working hacks?

☆

This evening, instead of the usual session, there was an Academic *séance* under the direction of the Pontifical Academy of Sciences. Two distinguished scholars addressed the Synod: one, His Excellency Giovanni Battista Marini-Bettolo, of the University of Rome and the Catholic University of the Sacred Heart, spoke on the Environment; the other, His Excellency Járôme Lejeune of the University of Paris, on Genetics.

We were not favoured with any details of what was said. Media people's brains are notoriously under-average in size, and they could not be expected to understand what their Excellencies had to say. (Mind you, they are asked to digest a fair bit of theology from time to time).

I should like to discover what was said about the environment. As we in Ireland know, interest in such matters was, until recently, a Protestant eccentricity. Now that we've seen the light, how far are we prepared to go? Can we expect moral denunciations of crimes against rivers and plants and even the lesser citizens of the animal kingdom? (No, I was not referring to coursing).

Friday 9th October

The voice and witness of Latin America in the Synod deserve a book to themselves – as indeed do those of Africa and Asia. Which is, I suppose, only to say that one can't generalise about the Church in the world of today. And yet the whole point of an assembly like this is surely that the universal Church, listening to, and learning from the experience, the insights, the sufferings, the victories of the local churches, may come to some conclusions, some tentative articulation of some part or parts of Truth, some expression of what the Holy Spirit is saying to us. Much of what will be said will need 'translation' into individual cultures, but there will always be something of immediate, universal relevance.

This morning, as ever, one was stirred by voices from older revivified churches, like that of Honduras walking on 'new pathways' with its *Delegates of the Word of God,* and its basic communities – and from younger churches, as in Tanzania, where the basic community are trying 'to eradicate the residues of sin by direct attack on poverty, ignorance and disease'. Stirred too by the very different witness of the Eastern churches, with their great liturgical tradition involving all the people.

And so we return home. Ireland's first contribution to the Synod, somewhat delayed – through no fault of the speaker – was heard today. As usual, Cardinal Ó Fiaich was well received – much applause, some laughter and, judging from remarks heard afterwards, considerable respect for what he had to say. I should like to quote some of the more striking passages:

It would be unwise of us bishops not to listen to as many lay voices as possible, both those which criticise as well as those which are satisfied. There can sometimes be a wide divergence between the fine statements of principle in Church documents about the laity and the practice at ground level in the normal diocese or parish.

For instance the documents say that clergy and laity are equal in dignity through their Baptism but some voices would claim that if we are all part of the pilgrim Church travelling through this life on the way to eternity, we must be travelling in a train with first-class and second-class carriages. The clergy have the power, privileges and prestige – they are the 'giving Church', which dispenses grace and lays down the rules. The laity are the 'receiving Church', expected to be passive, obedient, the object of the clergy's pastoral activites . . .

Most parishes have lay-people who could carry out some of the work connected with parish administration but they are seldom given the chance to do so. 'We were never asked' is their constant complaint.

The clergy (including the bishops) are slow to face the risk of dialogue or of sharing responsibility. They are no more willing to transfer part of their work than they would be to transfer part of their diocese to a neighbouring bishop. The laity are equally slow to come forward. Don't try to decide which side is most at fault. When one recalls the high hopes of twenty years ago, it is sad to have to admit that the laity in most parishes are still a largely untapped resource.

To animate the laity on a large scale we must first animate the priests on a large scale, and to animate the priests we must first animate the bishops, which will, I hope, be one of the results of this Synod . .

Finally a few words about the role of women:

Whether we like it or not feminism is now a challenge facing the Church. It can no longer be written off as middle-class madness or an American aberration. Unfortunately a considerable amount of alienation from the Church has already affected women in several countries. I'm not sure if we bishops realise how great is the anger of some who were once our friends. It will not be enough henceforth to issue grand statements unless we show progress in action. But at least we can carry out certain small things now to prevent further damage being done . . .

Finally, whenever we appoint women to ecclesiastical posts in the future, let us appoint them, when qualified, to the same types of work as men – teaching of theology, directors of retreats, members of Roman Congregations, and so on instead of confining their work to making the tea, sweeping the floor and arranging the flowers . . .

Comment is hardly necessary. Still, I was happy to hear the Cardinal urge his fellow-bishops to listen not alone to the happy laity but to those who criticise (shades of *Pobal!*); his animadversions on the 'giving church'/'receiving church' dichotomy were well taken, as was his recognition that 'large scale animation' of the laity must be preceded by similar 'animation' first of the bishops and then of the priests; and his 'few words about the role of women' were excellent. Clearly he sees no limit to that role in the non-cultic side of the Church — and I would be surprised if he were a hard-liner on ordination.

What the Cardinal had to say was warmly commended by Bishop Jean-Guy Hamelin of Rouyn-Noranda (Canada), who is also worth quoting at some length:

> The question of the participation of women in the life of the Church is a question of primary importance for the life and future of our Church.
>
> First task: *agree to look at the reality.* The movement of affirmation of women constitutes a fact characterising present social evolution, a 'sign of the times' (John XXIII).
>
> Second task: *exercise discernment.* This movement carries seeds for the humanisation of society, but it also carries risks of deviations. We are in the middle of a collective effort of discernment to be followed with openness and perseverance.
>
> Another task: *recognise and accompany this movement* which is breathing inside our Church. For this, it is necessary to open concrete paths:
>
> - Call for and recognise the contribution of Christian women in the vital debates of society: peace, bioethics, violence, family, etc.
> - Call for and recognise, in fact and by right, the full participation of women in ecclesial life: their voice is essential to the sacramentality of the Church and to her witness.
> - Remove canonical obstacles that block the access of laypersons to positions which do not require ordination (pastoral councils, tribunals, etc.).
> - Repeal regulations which exclude women from service at the altar and open the ministries of acolyte and lector to women.

From the preparatory consultation, we see that the question of women's access to ordained ministries remains controversial. One notices that the arguments used until now to limit ordination to men are not convincing, particularly to the young. It is suggested that there be set up, in individual interested churches, study groups for this question, gathering together men, women, pastors, and male and female theologians.

Access to the diaconate could represent a special case. Could we not recognise the charitable services of women present for centuries to the poverty and to daily service (homes, schools, hospitals, missions, etc.)?

Full participation of women is not a new need. It is the intuition of Genesis. There is no humanity that conforms to the heart of God without the coalition of man and woman.

After all that, it was interesting to hear another view, from Father Thomas Forrest, an American Redemptorist nominated to the Synod by the Pope. He didn't take an anti-feminist line, but he gently reminded his listeners that MEN are or should be a matter of deep concern too. In the USA about forty per cent of 'faithful churchgoers' are men, and it's even worse elsewhere. He went on to say that priests can spend so much time working for, or with, women that they become shy and insecure when called on to 'pastor' men: because it is easier to win response from women, a priest may tragically confine his ministry to them.

It would be foolish to deny that he has a point. One doesn't have to cross the Atlantic or even the Irish Sea to find the Church regarded as 'a place for women'. However, I believe that this attitude (and consequent practice) belongs to a dying sub-culture, deriving from a time when women had few other places to go outside the home. It may be cold comfort to say that today agnosticism and indifferentism are nearly as common among young women as among young men. As to priests' communication with men as against women, I suspect that the situation derived from regarding the priest as a 'safe' sexless thing. Though it didn't always work that way.

Considerably less persuasive to Irish ears was the summary we received of Cardinal Bernardin Gantin's contribution — or rather the first part of it. The second part was perfectly acceptable and timely dealing as it did with the world's 'wanderers' — '50 million emigrants, 15 million refugees, 10 million sailors, 15 million nomads' . . . No, it was the Cardinal's opening remarks that made me, for one, want to say: 'You're joking of course'. I quote from the summary:

On behalf of the Congregation of Bishops [of which he is Prefect] the Cardinal . . . indicated a new and very difficult and important question for the life of the Church: the part the laity can play in the requesting and furnishing of information with regard to candidates to the episcopate.

Canon 377 (3) provides for the eventual consultation of lay persons of outstanding wisdom in sworn secrecy. Such information is gathered with respect and careful consideration by the legitimate authorities: in fact, this participation of the laity is not considered a formal honour, but a true call and a duty of great importance . . .

My comment on this will be brief and restrained.

We in the Church of Dublin are not unaware of the provisions of Canon 377: it has been frequently cited since the death of Archbishop McNamara in spring of this year. We know that consultation of the laity is completely at the discretion of the Nuncio. I for one have never met anyone who was so consulted. But then, as I've already suggested, maybe I don't know the right people – particularly those of 'outstanding wisdom' . . .

The final speaker this evening was the Bishop of Down and Connor. He spoke of the struggle for peace and justice as a field marked by the 'sign of secularity and belonging in a special way to the laity:

I shall speak first of political activity. Political involvement is not as greatly esteemed as it should be by many and particularly by young people. It is highly important that men and women, inspired by their Christian faith and urged on by the love of Christ, should engage themselves in politics and should find here their own Christian vocation and indeed their own call to holiness. They must of course be careful not to identify the faith of the Church with any political option; but rather they should evaluate all political programmes by the light of the Gospel and strive to permeate them with Gospel values.

Women too must take their place in political activity. Society too often belittles their dignity and pays too little attention to their rights and their welfare. it is to be hoped that through the beneficial influence of women in politics society may come to assume a more human face, may show true respect for the sanctity of human life, may defend the rights of infants and of children, and may pursue a genuine politics of the family.

Among the truly grave political problems of our time a prominent place belongs to the untiring search for peace. Inseparably connected with this is the intense and persevering pursuit of justice. Sad to say there are many today who attempt to take the noble name of justice and to annex it for an ideology of revolutionary violence. But the fruit of violence is only to intensify oppression and to increase injustice. The so-called 'armed struggle for liberation' becomes itself a new instrument of injustice. We who live in the North of Ireland can state this with all the greater conviction because we have had nearly twenty years of sad experience of the effects of violence.

For many centuries a false glamourisation of war exercised a fatal fascination on the mind of generation after generation of people. This false glamour has now at last been, so to say, 'demythologised'. Regrettably at the same time another myth has been developed, namely the glamourisation of the so-called 'armed struggle for liberation'. This myth too is in urgent need of being 'demythologised' . . .

In order to operate competently in the political sphere lay persons need an appropriate formation. This formation must obviously include the sciences and the techniques of politics, the social sciences and economics and so forth. But above all a spiritual and biblical formation is required, so that political and social action may be motivated and guided by a truly evangelical spirit. There can be no genuine human liberation except in the Gospel of Jesus Christ . . .

Bishop Daly's appeal for political involvement and activity reminded me of a similar call by the Pope on his visit to Ireland in 1979, when he referred to politics as a 'noble profession', and suggested that violence was an inevitable consequence of the political vacuum. The Bishop's own vigorously expressed views on violence in the name of justice have implications going far beyond the island of Ireland. It will be interesting to see if they evoke any dissenting voices – from South Africa, say, or Central America. At the very least, no one can deny his authority to speak on this matter.

As to the other speakers this evening, I will content myself once again with some brief quotes:

Unjust structures can only be changed by a change of heart.

Bishop Quezada Toruno, Guatemala

We must provide more spaces in the Church to promote participation at all levels of lay commitment.

Bishop Morera Véga, Costa Rica

Our 'yes' to the world and its demands must be in harmony with our 'yes' to God. In this sphere, the laity are called to collaborate with persons of different convictions while remaining faithful to their Christian faith.

Bishop Werbs, German Democratic Republic

There are many in the Church who still have a very 'disincarnate' faith' and for whom the social, economic and political areas appear as something foreign to their being Christian . . . The *preferential option for the poor* is for the Church as a whole . . . As Pope John Paul said: 'The poor are unable to hope'.

Bishop Ariztia Ruiz, Chile

A synodal call to holiness . . . runs the risk of being understood as a 'supernatural escape' . . . Let us rather propose a notion of sanctity which is the opposite of an invitation to leave this world and seek union with God elsewhere.

Bishop Lescrauwaet, The Netherlands

True hierarchical communion and discipleship are first experienced in the liturgy. From the liturgical assembly the faithful are to go forth as sons and daughters of the Lord to transform the world.

Archbishop Powathil, India

There must be *just as much* concern for the formation of the laity as for the formation of candidates to the priesthood. It need not be academic: it must be born of the joy of living as Christians without the feeling of being exploited . . . *Professional competence* is essential if Christian witness is to be a true sign to the world.

Archbishop Fernandes de Araujo, Brazil

One other speaker should be noted, not so much for what he said as for what he represents. This is Monsignor Luigi Guissani of *Communione e Liberazione,* an organisation to which I have already referred and of which we will be hearing much more very shortly. His name, by the way, is on the list of Papal nominees to the Synod.

Saturday 10th October

This morning's session heard contributions from several 'stars' of the Synod – Cardinal Hume of Westminster; Cardinal Etchegaray, who is President of the Pontifical Commission for Justice and Peace (and of the Pontifical Council *Cor Unum); Cardinal Ballestrero of Turin; and Vatican II veteran, Archbishop Mark McGrath of Panama. All of them said good things – especially, perhaps, Cardinal Etchegaray, who spoke of the Church-World relationship as 'always unstable, never perfect'. Human values are 'weighed down with ambiguity: it is up to the Church to give them their full meaning'. He reminded us that 'eschatology is not a reality of tomorrow; it is an experience of today.'

But for me the most memorable and substantial of the session's contributions – indeed one of the most remarkable heard since the Synod began – was that of Bishop John Sherlock of London (Ontario) one of the four representatives of the Canadian Episcopal Conference. I have no hesitation in quoting his summary in full.

The split between culture and the Gospel is 'the drama of our time'. Traditional cultures, organised around religion, are in full retreat before a new culture which assigns to religion an unimportant private corner.

Recent Popes have advocated that lay Christians learn to 'read the signs of the times', and involve themselves directly in the complex, ambiguous process of the transformation of culture. This can only be done in collaboration with others, including non-believers.

Lay Christians are everywhere in this global culture. God's Spirit helps them to discern the seeds of life and the seeds of death in the world. Such discernment in faith is ordered to action in the world. It is an inspired prudence. We struggle in Canada to act discerningly and socially, in coalitions with fellow-citizens who are shapers of culture, and in solidarity with suffering people.

The recent visit of the Holy Father to Fort Simpson highlights one area where a shared work towards cultural justice for aboriginal peoples has been under way for a long time. It has made possible a particularly 'incarnated' proclamation of Christ.

We now believe that it is in such a process of *involvement, discernment,* and *negotiation* that Catholic social teaching must be forged. Its formulation requires not just a statement of church principles but 'the contribution of all charisms, experiences and skills'. (*Instruction on Christian Freedom and Liberation,* no. 72.)

I would ask the Synod to foster this way of practical discernment through action in the world, in faith, as a common way of Christian formation. I would ask that this way of developing Catholic social teaching become normative at all levels of Church life.

For lay Catholics, this mission of transforming the world, of breathing Spirit into the world, is not a power game. It progresses by the way of the Cross. It identifies the laity profoundly with Jesus' own crucified self-giving. The least we can do is to offer those brothers and sisters of ours our own lives, as pastors. And the first gift we can offer is our willingness to listen and to learn.

One need not accept every word of Bishop Sherlock's analysis to recognise its rare quality of realism and vision. It is not the least of several outstanding contributions made by the Canadian church to the church universal over the past twenty-five years.

I must however quote from one more of this morning's interventions, that of His Beatitude Stephanos II Ghattas, Patriarch of Alexandria of the Copts. In reference to the 'specifically important part' played by the *lay faithful* in the churches of the East, not least that of the Copts, he had this to say:

Aware of their baptismal character and of the obligation that they had of preaching the Good News . . *they were missionaries to foreign countries,* according to the example of the early Christians. Think simply, by way of example, of Ireland and Switzerland evangelised by the Egyptian soldiers of the Theban legion . . .

Well, now! Mind you, I remember the Coptic observer at Vatican II, when I told him I was Irish, remarking 'Ah! yes: the Irish. We converted you, of course.'

Of course. That's why so many of us think of the Church as *pyramid* . . .

No session this evening. But don't imagine it was all golf, football matches, and visits to the cinema. Far from it. All the Synod members, including the auditors, were taken off to visit Roman parishes.

As for me, I settled for afternoon tea. Or something.

Sunday 11th October

On this morning, twenty-five years ago, Pope John XXIII, of happy memory, presided at the opening of the Second Vatican Council. Those of us who were there – as Council Fathers, *periti* or mere journalists and allied riff-raff, are now getting thin on the ground, and not quite as young as we used to be.

There were, I imagine, a few moist eyes in St Peter's this morning among those at the Commemorative Mass. And not a few ghosts. Two of them were remembered by name in the Roman Canon – John himself, and his great successor Paul VI – and, of all the others who were not named, each of us was thinking of the special ones we loved and worked with and argued against. And as we sang *Kyrie eleison* our prayer was for them all, for us all . . .

Not that my own 'dispositions' on that October morning 1962, the feast of the Motherhood of Mary in the old calendar, were altogether appropriate to the occasion. For one thing we had to be in St Peter's at the crack of dawn, hours before anything happened. Whether this was Vatican bloody-mindedness, or anxiety or for the good of our souls, I never found out. Nor why the 'tribune' that was supposed to accommodate journalists was three-quarters occupied by NUNS – a variety of them dressed in voluminous habits that are now probably museum pieces. By sheer brute force and ignorance, and refusing to take lip from the 'black' aristocracy who patrolled the Basilica (one learns quickly in Rome), I eventually squeezed into a corner which I shared sardine-like with, as I recall, the *Daily Express* (a devout Anglican), the *News of the World* (an old Downside boy) – both alas! no longer with us – and dear Molly McGee, then representing *The People*, who still flourishes, and I'm sure remembers Cardinal Newman as a small boy. Lest I should be completely

Anglicised by contiguity, I turned my eyes to another loftier tribune where among the foreign delegations I could just glimpse the Irish, lead, as I seem to remember, by the then Taoiseach, Seán Lemass.

But that was little help to a man with a hangover and no breakfast, nor indeed was the 'warm-up' by the Sistine Choir, members of whom, I couldn't help recalling, had got stuck, with their conductor Bartolucci, in a lift in the Shelbourne Hotel a couple of years before, while the old Theatre Royal, packed to its 4,000 seater capacity waited and waited – and this unfortunate commentator waffled and waffled into a microphone. (It all ended reasonably well.)

And then at long last the great procession entered the Basilica, over 2,000 strong, and, like all such processions, part impressive, part (because of all those bobbing mitres) slightly comic. My own memories of the beginning of the Liturgy are, as they say, fitful, but I do remember the beloved face of John as he sat in Peter's chair, like a mother hen with her chickens, as he looked with evident delight at the circle of guests who sat in places of high honour above all: the Observers from other Churches, of the East and of the West, whose presence was the tangible sign of a new Christian era, and the fulfilment of John's own ardent hope.

The pontifical liturgy continued in its stately Tridentine way. If my memory serves me right, Pope John was not the celebrant – 'presiding' without celebrating was quite common in those days. And, of course, only the celebrant (Cardinal Tisserant, I think, as Dean of the College of Cardinals) took Holy Communion. This would, thank God, be unthinkable now – at today's Mass everyone in the Basilica, I imagine, took part (also in the singing and the prayers) even though I have to say the method of bringing Communion to the people left much to be desired.

I have to confess that St. Peter's is not my favourite place of worship. Like the Church of the Holy Sepulchre in Jerusalem, Notre Dame in Paris, St Patrick's in Dublin, it attracts tourists who, with the best will in the world, can hardly be called pilgrims – not so much the Church in the World as the world in the church! (Who's being *élitiste* now?) . . . However it must be said that conciliar reform is triumphantly vindicated on occasions like today, when a Papal Mass is a genuine community celebration, stripped of the accretions of the past – many of them admittedly 'impressive' and, all in all, a splendid example of that 'notable simplicity' the Council sought.

At the beginning of the concelebration, Pope John Paul called for an acknowledgement of the many ways in which we have failed the vision of the Council: this was spelt out in three 'invocations', spoken by three of the concelebrants – one in French, one in Spanish, and one in English which declared:

. . . We have set out on an ecumenical path that in desire, in prayer and forgiveness seeks to embrace all the sons and daughters of our heavenly father. The road that leads to unity is long, tiresome, and requires patience and trust in God together with an evangelical love of our brothers and sisters. Too often we have become weary, and relied on merely human energies . . .

The first two readings were in Spanish and English, respectively; the Gospel (Matthew 22:2-24) was sung first in Latin and then in Greek (traditional in Papal Masses). The gospel book was then enthroned before the altar as it was – the very same book – during Vatican II *and* Vatican I.

The Pope for his homily took as his text the words of the psalmist, 'The Lord is My Shepherd'. He quoted John XXIII who insisted that the Church's 'certain and unchangeable doctrine, which must be faithfully respected, be deepened and presented in a way that corresponds to the needs of our time.' He went on to say:

All the Council documents did nothing more than to develop these suggestions offered by Pope John. The Council accomplished an immense work of reassuming the preceding doctrinal patrimony and, at the same time, drew up, on the basis of that patrimony, a vast programme of renewal which regards almost every area of Christian action, on the personal as well as on the communitarian level.

The teachings of the Council, rightly understood and interpreted in the context of the preceding Magisterium, can well be called the *plan of action for the Christian of our time.*

On this Sunday, we desire, therefore, to thank the Lord, the Good Shepherd, for the work carried out by Vatican II, inaugurated twenty five years ago.

In the course of these years, the Church, and in her individual communities have also experienced many trials. Many faithful had to 'walk in a dark valley', in the midst of various tribulations that were able to arouse in their souls sentiments of trepidation and fear.

Still the psalmist says: *'I will fear no evil, because you are with me.'*

Yes, the Lord is the true Shepherd. The Lord is our Shepherd. Amen.

At the Prayer of the Faithful, intercessions were offered in French, Fanti, Tamil, Ukrainian, German and Polish. The Council was again recalled twice during the Eucharistic Prayer, including, as I've already said, the *Memento* for the departed. And at the end we sang the *Magnificat,* to thank God and honour Mary . . .

But over and over again, memories of that first morning kept crowding in: memories of physical discomfort; an almost reluctant response to the grandeur of the ceremony; a certain scepticism (shared by many) about what it was all going to add up to (it was commonly believed that the proceedings were 'all sewn up in advance' by the Curia), struggling with an inescapable sense of occasion . . . and then, suddenly, in the twinkling of an eye, the great, clear trumpet-call from Peter's chair, as John aroused us from our torpor, bade us cast off fear, listen to the lessons of history, stop moaning and condemning, and go out into the world in the hope of the Holy Spirit – into his world and ours, and let our light shine before men.

It was the end of an age, the beginning of an age, a revolution, a leap into the future, a new call to faith and hope and love . . .

For what we have failed to do, *Kyrie eleison.*

Monday 12th October

Good news this morning! This is to be the final day of general discussion in plenary session: There will in fact be two such sessions tomorrow, the morning being given over to the auditors, and the afternoon to Cardinal Thiandoum's second *Relatio* . . . I say good news, because I believe it was generally felt inside and outside the Synod that more than enough formal statements had been heard, and that the sooner the Fathers got down to work in the smaller groups the better. Still, everyone entitled and wanting to speak had to be heard: so it was announced the other day that the lists would close at the weekend. With, it is clear, good effect.

I mentioned that on Friday evening the Synod heard from the representative of *Communione e Liberazione.* This morning's first speaker was Monsignor Alvaro del Portillo, Prelate of *Opus Dei* – another Papal nominee. These two organisations are perhaps the best-known and (blessed word!) controversial of the several 'movements' which have come to prominence in the Church of our time. (Our own Legion of Mary is, of course, another.)

The word 'movement' has in fact become one of the buzz-words of the Synod, not alone in relation to 'Opus' and 'Communione', but because of certain questions touching the structures of jurisdiction and authority in the Church. Some regard them with enthusiasm, others with considerable reserve. It would however be very wrong to regard the arguments on either side as purely 'institutional' in the narrow sense: even in matters of organisational autonomy *vis-à-vis* the local church, far deeper issues are involved – issues touching the nature of the Church, evangelical and pastoral issues, response to the Spirit, 'discernment of charisms' and so on.

I have avoided this topic until now, not least because the third session with the auditors – now taking place tomorrow – has been signalled as dealing with it in, presumably, a fairly detailed manner. There have indeed been several interventions on the subject since the opening of the Synod, but perhaps what Cardinal Martini of Milan had to say this morning can be regarded as a judicial summing-up:

> I wish to speak of the new associations and movements in the Church (see *Instrumentum Laboris,* nn. 59-60) in the context of Italy and Europe. The Holy Father has spoken to the European Bishops more than once of the need for a new quality of evangelisation in Europe. It is a question of proclaiming the Gospel in a climate of growing secularisation.
>
> Though she, too, finds herself in this general context, the Church in Italy can today count on many lively forces. Besides the major traditional associations (e.g. Catholic Action, the Scouts), we find at the base of our parishes very many groups, both organised and not, whose action is incisive and efficacious. In Italy there are also many associations which are referred to as 'new', insofar as they were born or have grown in recent decades. These are very different one from another, and it is almost impossible to treat them all under one common denominator. They are committed and capable of arousing enthusiasm. Our principal pastoral duty before these new realities is discernment, which means not only evaluation and judgement, but also accompaniment over time. Such discernment is the responsibility first of all of pastors

but also of the group members themselves, who must let themselves be assisted in better understanding the ways of the Lord for the service of the one Church.

The particular Church, in the communion of the churches, is the natural place for the discernment of the path chosen by a movement. This is all the more necessary where movements have specifically pastoral goals and involve the Christian presence in society.

The faithful have the right freely to found associations with religious, charitable or apostolic aims (Canon 299). But this itself does not guarantee the evangelical value and the Christian authenticity of these entities. Furthermore, every association or movement necessarily places itself in the context of a particular Church, in which it is the bishop's responsibility to plan, promote and unify the pastoral activity of the diocese. To the degree that an association or a movement represents a real and recognised good for the particular Church, it should be sustained for the values and enrichment that it brings, as long as it is disposed to the process of discernment and docile in letting itself be accompanied on the path towards a more organic form of ecclesiastical discipline.

The Cardinal's view was also echoed very succinctly by Bishop Mendes de Almeide (a Jesuit like the Cardinal) from Brazil.

Christian associations and groups, when they place their gifts and charisms at the service of communion, bring about the growth of the whole people of God; when, instead, they close in upon themselves they can be detrimental to the whole ecclesial body.

Also from Brazil, Archbishop Colling of Porto Alegre said:

Autonomous movements or pastoral ministries which do not have a real link with the Church must take responsibility for their own success or lack of success.

It should be noted, by the way, that the last two bishops named, and indeed many, many others, refer approvingly to another kind of organisation, the basic christian community. This seems now to be taken for granted, and not only in the Third World, as a way of bringing new life to the local church from within. (It was, as I recall, given a general blessing at the Synod on Evangelisation.)

Before leaving this morning's session I must mention two more voices from the Third World, both from countries torn by civil war. The Archbishop of Khartoum in the Sudan spoke of

> . . . the kind of Islam that is propagated by force, deceit and injustice; that is used as an instrument of oppression, exploitation and political power; that disregards human dignity and rights . . .

and of a

> . . . poverty which by reducing many to live in conditions unworthy of human beings has deprived them also of their sense of being human . . .

And the Bishop of Santiago de Maria (El Salvador) had a word of hope, long-deferred, based on the recent Central-American Peace Plan:

> The accord . . . and the dialogue between the Governor of El Salvador and the rebels, which took place in the Nunciature, with His Excellency Archbishop Artura Rivera Lamas acting as mediator, with all the results these have already achieved, have awoken in our long-suffering people a very real hope of peace.

This evening's is the last scheduled plenary session involving general interventions by the Fathers. However, some have not yet spoken, so we may have a few tomorrow morning.

☆

I have referred to the fact that some of the Third World speakers chose Latin – one of these was the first to be heard this evening, Archbishop Saen-Phon-On of Thailand. He recalled that 'Buddhimus in Thailandia religio nationalis recognoscitur' and that the small Catholic minority have frequently been in difficulties: indeed, in 1940, seven were martyred *'propter odium fidei'*. And still this small minority seems to have considerable influence. Recently a move by the government to legalise abortion 'legalisare abortum' was opposed by a Catholic medical-lay coalition who conducted their campaign so successfully that the proposed legislation never appeared 'legislatio illa nunquam apparuerat!'

From Malawi, the Bishop of Dedza tells of a laity who seem to be able to turn their hands to everything:

> With the new teaching of Vatican II in mind, the laity in Malawi are all out to play their role in the church. They take up their role

at every level of the diocesan setting. They are in pastoral councils, parish councils and church councils. They assume responsibilities in the small christian communities. They assume such roles as Sunday prayer leaders. These conduct prayer-services on Sundays or feasts of obligation in the absence of the priest. There are voluntary teachers among them who teach first communicants and confirmandi. They also teach catechumens in their various groups. They give instructions to those who are getting married. There are choir leaders who prepare and conduct the singing during the Mass or Sunday prayer services. It is the laity who join and keep alive the different movements in the Church.

On the material level, we note with satisfaction that the laity are more than ever before carrying out self-help projects. They put up school blocks, build teachers' houses, plant trees for timber and firewood but also for soil conservation. They dig wells for clean water.

The Church's option for the poor, solidarity and identification and communion with them must now be shown in being united with their spirit and power for non-violence. A strong programme of non-violence on the part of the Church will sustain people's non-violence. Non-violence is so urgent and challenging that both clergy, laity and religious in the Church and people of goodwill of other religions and cultures will join hands and forces together in the task. This itself will bring communion in the Church and other peoples.

Non-violence heals the hardness of heart that comes from violence. It brings also a spirit of reconciliation. Our many devoted priests will find in the programmes of non-violence a way of calling people to penance and reconciliation.

And from India, Archbishop Padijara, speaks of the 'missionary' duty of the laity:

Only Christians who live in Jesus can attract their fellow men to Christ. Conversions are made not by syllogisms but by prayer, charism and witnessing the faith.

The laity who are active in politics and other public affairs have an obligation to give testimony to their faith. The indifference of the good people is the cause of the victory of the wicked. When justice, freedom, religious or human rights are violated and trampled upon in public life, let the laity speak aloud. Politics,

66

good or bad, affects everybody. This is the time for the laity to come forward and to spread the message of Christ in the world . . .

Tuesday 13th October

I was right in my guess that this morning's session might include a few final interventions from the Fathers. There were in fact four, all of them interesting. Once again, an Indian Archbishop, this time the Metropolitan of Trivandrum of the Syro-Malankarese, brought very old and very new together in linking the ancient liturgical piety of the laity, with their desperate current economic and social needs. He suggested 'Health for All by A.D. 2000' as a target.

The new century was also the preoccupation of Archbishop Tonini of Ravenna-Cervia. He looked forward to the impending 'globalisation' of all human realities, and specifically to the likely 'Islamisation of Europe' due to a falling birth-rate. In the future then, the term 'salvation' will take on 'an ever fuller and more radical meaning, one embracing the whole destiny of individuals and peoples'.

From Cuba, the Synod heard Bishop Pena Gomez of Holguin. The circumstances of the Church there make his report of especial interest.

During the '60s lay organisations diminished, but a very active participation on the part of the laity in intra-ecclesial life was growing. Results of this progress:

- A laity well integrated into the community and united to their pastors.
- Lay services or lay ministries with which we cannot dispense, especially because of the scarcity of pastoral workers.
- Silent testimony in front of the commitments of life and of the individual apostolate.
- Pastoral councils.

This present situation matured, expressed itself and was projected in the entire reflective process which culminated in the Cuban National Ecclesial Meeting, Havana, February, 1986, (and still continues).

The Church in Cuba will concentrate her major efforts on being a more evangelising Church, more a Church of prayer, more incarnate in an attitude of dialogue.

This orientation is not foreign to the laity; but it is the laity, for the most part, who with their fidelity to the Church and to their people made it possible.

There follow these options for the Cuban Church:

- New areas of evangelisation as a specific service to our people, through ecclesial communion, are opening to the awareness of the Cuban laity.
- At this time proposals for the lay apostolate are taking shape, based on the following criteria:
  - ecclesial communion
  - promotion of the commitment of laity in the community.
  - the institution of some lay services as ministries is being looked at.

We live with Mary, in hope.

☆

Father John Vaughn OFM, Minister General of the Order of Friars Minor, spoke of the historic 'Third' or Secular Orders, associated with the great religious families:

Some of the great masters of Christian life gave inspiration not only to groups of religious, but also to groups of laity, not to make them semi-cloistered, but to offer them the same deep experience of God as is available to priests and religious, but in the world, and precisely as lay people:

as married couples
as professional people
as people involved in political life.

In turn, these lay people have prolonged and extended to the Church and the world the charism of their own religious family through a form of secular spirituality and involvement. The structure of these Third or Secular Orders, and similar associations, has enabled the charism of the founder to be preserved by association with a religious family which offers spiritual assistance. But the Secular Order is distinct from, and complementary to, the religious order, and its leadership is in the hands of the laity who in communion with their pastors, exercise their own proper gifts to build up the Church and evangelise society.

The Secular Orders have renewed their legislation and structures in the light of the Second Vatican Council: this renewal stresses the dignity of the laity's vocation, their right and need to assume responsibility, and the rightful autonomy of their action in the Church and in society.

This was an appropriate link with the second half of the session in which lay speakers addressed the Synod on 'The Life of Associations and Movements'.

'May a hundred flowers bloom!' I don't know whether Mr Guzman Carriquiry from Uruguay who is an Assistant to the Special Secretary of the Synod, and has been described to me as the highest placed layman in the Curia, used this phrase with a straight face, when he wished that the 'beauty of the gifts and experiences' of the great variety of associations in today's Church would enrich the community in unity. (Not that the Age of the Laity is to be compared with a certain Cultural Revolution.)

His address could be read as an enthusiastic *apologia* for associations and movements. Having saluted 'Catholic Action' (do you remember? . . .), he pointed to the new organisations recognised by the present Pope as 'fruits of the Spirit and reasons for hope'.

They can be characterised by several aspects:

- Their emerging and surprising newness, not 'programmed', as signs of the liberty of forms with which the one Church is realised.
- Their growth in ecclesial land cultivated by the Council and in a phase of planting and growth of its good fruits.
- The tonality which is more charismatic than 'functional'.
- Their reality as 'ecclesial' movements rather than 'lay', and the transition from 'theologies of the laity' to ecclesiology of communion.
- Their 'in-put' which is more missionary than 'ecclesiastic'.

The next speaker was an old friend, Jerzy Turowicz from Cracow, pioneer and father-figure of the *Znak* organisation, which fulfilled the promise of its name – it means 'Sign' – in some of Poland's most difficult years since its foundation in 1948.

I first met him during the Council: a gentle intellectual, committed to the Church, but with a sharp critical sense and an equally sharp sense of humour. He has been a frequent visitor to Rome since then – except when petty tyranny at home prevented his leaving. Over the last decade, however, prudence has no doubt dictated a more diplomatic approach to this independent-minded man who has also been a close friend of Pope John Paul for many years. He was absent from the 1985 Synod, but for reasons of health: he confessed to me the other day that it finally persuaded him to give up smoking!

His work with *Znak* has been mainly, though not altogether, as a publisher and journalist – frustrated from time to time by a 'shortage' of paper, sometimes genuine, sometimes contrived. Such shortage seemed less frequently to affect the publications of *Pax,* the fellow-travelling Catholic.

It should be said, however, that Turowicz seemed always to be regarded with respect and affection, not alone by *Pax* journalists at the Council, but also by government news agency personnel. Later, on my own short time in Poland in 1977, I sensed the same regard for one whose writings have always been marked by honesty, restraint and balance, as well as considerable courage.

His intervention this morning, in style and content, came as no surprise to anyone who had read those careful but unambiguous reflections of his, usually cyclostyled on the vilest of newsprint. His subject now was 'The Laity in the Parish', and he clearly sees the traditional parochial unit as full of potential for the future, and the natural nucleus for development. As to the 'great debate', as ever, a balanced line:

> Sometimes the parish is opposed as an institutional structure of the Church, in the lay movements which would be part of her charismatic structure. Now this opposition is without foundation. These two aspects of the Church should be inseparably linked rightly in the heart of the parish.
>
> The most natural path of this transformation of the parish lies in the pastoral councils suggested by Vatican II. It is with such a council – composed of laity, men and women – that the pastor ought to share the responsibility for everything that concerns the parish: pastoral, spiritual, economic problems, etc.
>
> In each parish there are the poor, the lonely, the elderly, the abandoned. If the parish is to be a community of love and of sharing, each person in need ought not to be taken for granted. It

would rightly be the task of the laity to reach those persons. The care of the poor must also embrace the spiritually poor: wounded by life, strayed, the marginated, who generally remain outside the field of action of the parish. However, the Church must take care of them. This is also the laity's area of action.

The problem of missionary involvement of the laity is broader than the parish framework. But it is the Eucharist which is the source of this involvement. Now, it is the parish which is the privileged place where a lay person, in union with the community to which he belongs, ought to participate in the Eucharistic celebration.

Twenty years after Vatican II in some churches there still are not pastoral councils, neither at the diocesan level nor at the parish level. We have the right to wish that one of the fruits of this Synod of Bishops be the creation of these councils in all parishes of all individual churches.

From another troubled country, El Salvador, Ms Lilian de Perez (again not on the list of auditors) spoke mainly of Basic Communities (CEB): these have been developing in the Archdiocese of San Salvador since the 60s and were given official status in 1970. She went on to say:

In 1972, as a consequence of the current repression, there was a conscientisation at social level, giving origin to political choices, with the setting up of Popular Organisations. In this social frame, Archbishop Monsignor Oscar Arnulfo Romero is to be mentioned, who marked his pastoral approach in such a way that it led to his martyrdom. *Still now his person is very highly exalted in the political field, more than as a pastor consistent with his mission.* (Third Pastoral Letter, Monsignor Arturo Rivers Damas).

The last sentence, which I have italicised, is open to more than one reading: perhaps it's a matter of translation, though I don't think so. What a pity Bishop Éamonn Casey isn't here . . .

One gathers from what Ms Perez has to say that the CEB story also involves certain ambiguities: leading to 'politicisation without conversion' on the one hand, and on the other, a 'flight-from-the-world' kind of spiritual emphasis. Still, she believes that such communities 'in the sense in which they are understood by the Magisterium' are *totally necessary* (unlike the 'Apostolic Movements' which she merely describes as an 'efficacious way of bringing people

71

together'). She believes that, from the basic community

> . . . there flows a total pastoral involvement which, in turn, will give rise to new generations to struggle to bring about radical social change, based on the Gospel.

But both clergy, who act *in persona Christi,* and laity, need a 'constant renewal of mind and heart'.

Mr Raabe of the Federal Republic of Germany took as his theme 'Unity and Coordination of Lay Activities at the National Level', and stressed that lay participation is not limited to family life, the parish or the diocese. He clearly sees 'movements' and other associations as of importance nationally:

> The coordination of all the forces of the Catholic laity at the national level is important also for political reasons. The political realm, especially in states with democratic institutions, is the forum in which there takes place the great social dialogue . . . Catholic citizens must not be missing from this realm; they associate to defend their Christian vision of society and so to contribute to the common good. Their voice will acquire more power and importance if they come forward together, if they speak with one voice and are able to act in unity.
>
> In a pluralistic society, the great social dialogue is an unrenounceable prerequisite for freedom. The future of the world belongs to pluralism, notwithstanding all the hindering or even totalitarian elements at work.

The two final auditors who spoke were women. Ms Genevieve Rivière from France, on 'The Mission of the Laity in International Life', made special reference to

> . . . International Catholic bodies [which] are, for the most part, recognised as non-governmental organisations by the United Nations, with a consultative status which permits them to be heard at international level in order to denounce injustices, defend human rights and promote the human development of peoples . . .

Ms Rivière is described as President of the Conference of International Catholic Organisations.

Her fellow-auditor, Ms Chiara Lubich, is foundress of the *Focolare* movement in Italy. Her subject was 'The Spirituality of the Laity and of Movements' and she appeared to have no doubt that 'through movements, the Holy Spirit is arousing spiritualities, firmly rooted in the Gospel, which help the laity in a special way to live as authentic Christians in today's secularised environment', and that these laity respond by 'committing themselves to doing his will in the concreteness of daily life'.

As she developed her theme – 'striving to love Christ in the persons with whom they have contact'; 'reciprocal love is translated into the communion of material, cultural and spiritual goods'; 'evangelisation is facilitated, conversions to the faith and vocations mature, and dialogue with other Christians . . . with all men [sic] becomes more fruitful' – I had to ask myself, as often before: 'Isn't this simply about being a Christian? Why the emphasis on "joining" something? Isn't it enough to be in the Church?' Nor do I find it any great help to be told that:

> In today's de-christianised world, the Spirit, *through movements,* underlines a particular presence of Christ: where two or three are gathered in his name (see *Mt 18:20*), there unity is realised . . .   [*my italics*]

Reminding us that one must 'make the mystery of the Cross one's own', Ms Lubich tells us that 'other elements in the spiritual life of today's committed Christians are 'love of the Eucharist and of the Hierarchy'(!) . . . and a 'deep rapport with Mary' oddly described as 'the first lay person' . . . *Leor san go fóill.*

☆

The workings of the Synod are, as they say, something else. I mean the mechanics. It's all set out in a document of some thirty closely-printed pages which (you will be glad to hear) I do not propose to include in this Diary. Neither can I offer a proper summary. The best way of grasping the procedure is to look at it in *three phases.*

- *Phase One*, you may recall, began on 2 October with a first *Relatio,* in which the 'Relator' or Moderator, Cardinal Thiandoum presented an over-view of the matters to be discussed, and indicated special problem areas to be addressed. It ended this evening with a second *Relatio,* which purported to sum up the work of the plenary sessions in which nearly all the Synod Fathers spoke in turn.

- *Relatio II* is also a link with the *Second Phase* of the Synod which begins tomorrow: from then until the weekend, discussion will be in the *circuli minores,* smaller groups (based on language), who will report back to plenary sessions on Monday and Tuesday next. Then the groups reform, this time to prepare specific proposals, which will be sifted and collated by the following weekend (with some plenary discussions).

● The *Third* and final *Phase* begins on Monday week next, 26 October: from then until the last session on Thursday, 29 October, the Fathers will consider, discuss, amend and finally vote on the proposals which will be incorporated into a collated document for presentation to the Pope. (Remember, the Synod is an advisory, not a decision-making, body.) They may also draw up a general statement message for general consumption.

That's as concise as I can make it. The second phase which we're now entering is, in many ways, the most interesting, although the ideas which emerge from the various groups will not surface until they report back next Monday.

As to *Relatio II* we were issued this evening with a summary which was as meaty as a well-picked chicken carcass. However, with the help of the diligent and long-suffering Diarmuid it is possible to provide some idea of the document which is (as ever!) divided into three parts.

The first deals with the theology and ecclesiology of *communio*: the laity as *Christifideles,* the common priesthood and that of orders, communion and mission, the 'secular' character of laity, the fundamental action of the Holy Spirit calling all to one holiness, but conferring a variety of charisms.

The second section on 'Unity and Pluriformity' looks at the Church, local and catholic; parishes and basic communities; movements, associations and religious orders; ministries.

The third part considers 'Contemporary Changes and Dynamisms' of the Church in the world: lay action in family, politics, culture; lay formation; the position of women, young adults and children; 'formation' and spirituality.

It all appears rather blandly inclusive, although I gather there were some voices raised complaining of omissions. In any event it's up to the working groups to tease it out, fill in what's missing, and tear all or any part of it up. And, of course, matters can still be raised which were not mentioned at all so far . . . So, end of phase one.

Wednesday 14th October

There are, it appears, twelve *circuli minores*. One will work in Italian, three in French, three in Spanish (and Portuguese), one in German and three in English. Oh, yes! And one in Latin.

Where there is more than one group for a language, those taking part are divided alphabetically. Thus in English group A the name *Daly* (Cahal B.) is flanked by *d'Souza* (Henry S.) and *de Lastic* (Alan Basil) — both from India. *Ó Fiaich* (Tomás) heads the list for English group C, closely followed by *Onaiyekan* (John O.) — from Nigeria — and *Ott* (Stanley J.) of Baton Rouge, USA . . .Talk about group dynamics!

By the way, looking down the lists one is struck by how few Irish names there are, compared, say, to the Council years when they seemed to be all over the place. A large number of these were from Africa, and their near disappearance is surely the best possible tribute to how well those Irish missionaries did their work.

I should say that all the lists (except the Latin one) include names of auditors: *Fay* (Patrick) is in English group A, and *Sweeney* (Walter) — a permanent deacon from New York in group C . . . The Latin group, incidentally, is very small indeed: a mere five names, including Cardinal Vaivods of Latvia (USSR) — and, sadly, Monsignor Hirka of Czechoslovakia who has been prevented from attending.

Suddenly, the Sala Stampa has become very quiet, as many correspondents have gone home — some to return for the final week. For those who remain, it's the time for 'think pieces', as they're called in the trade, which are the reluctant journalist's substitute for hard, or hardish, news. So everybody was glad to go to hear Monsignor Vincent Nicholls, who is Secretary to the Bishops' Conference of England and Wales, give his opinion on how things are beginning to shape up. He didn't claim to have either inside information, or x-ray eyes to divine any 'hidden agenda', but what he had to say was clear and sensible, and helped to clarify things for many of us. He saw five main questions to be resolved, or, if not resolved, at least identified and developed:

- What is the laity?
- How does one define — or categorise — lay ministry (ministries)?

- How to 'place' the lay role in the Church and in the world?
- How to reach a consensus on the 'movements'?
- How to give substantial expression to the generally positive attitude to women?

I have not quoted Nicholls verbatim, but that's more or less what he said.

Plenty of scope for 'think pieces' there, and one could (even without x-ray eyes) see them beginning to take shape in several busy minds.

We were gathered under the auspices of the excellent *Pro Mundi Vita* [PMV] organisation: they are an international research and information centre with headquarters in Brussels, and located for the duration of the Synod at the Augustinianum which is close (geographically, at least) to what used to be the Holy Office. PMV provide documentation and secretarial services, as well as a forum for discussion each afternoon, centred on a talk, given on alternate days in English and in French. Most of the centre's personnel are, I think, Belgian, but they do include the redoubtable Willy Jenkinson CSSp, sometime Irish Provincial of his congregation.

The PMV's services and 'fringe events' are in worthy succession to those provided during Vatican II by CCCC, an organisation the meaning of whose initials I'm afraid I've forgotten, and also by DOC which was run by a remarkable Dutch priest Leo Alting von Geusau on behalf of his country's bishops. That was where it all happened – well some of it, anyway . . .

Mention of the CCCC reminds me of a colleague who said the 'four Cs' made *him* think of the four things he disliked most about Rome: *cars* (even in the 60s they were lethal); *coffee machines* (the noise they made, he said, 'especially in the morning'); *campari* which he described as a drink 'fit only for civil servants'; and *clerics*. On the last of these, I gathered that what he found objectionable was what he called their 'black petticoats', in other words the soutanes which, along with those curious hats with their oddly Anglican appearance, 'made normal young men look like transvestites'. If he were here today he would be hard put to it to find his *bêtes noirs*: in fact I can imagine him complaining that he couldn't tell cleric from lay, in a world of sweaters and jeans. A point not without relevance to our Synodal concerns.

Mind you, the Romans themselves aren't bad at re-interpreting initials. Take, for instance SPQR, which you'll find all over the city, on everything from dustbin lids and manhole covers to the doors of municipal offices and civic monuments. It is of course, slightly pretentiously, taken from the ancient *Senatus Populusque Romanus* – the 'Senate and People of Rome' – proud title of a proud community.

But the Romans aren't content to leave it at that. SPQR, they say, asks a question: 'Sancte Pater Quare Rides' – *Holy Father, why are you laughing?* And they say, if you turn the letters around, you have the answer: RQPS – 'Rideo Quia Papa Sum' – *I'm laughing because I'm the Pope* . . .

Thursday 15th October

Of all the 'movements' we've been hearing so much about, *Communione e Liberazione* seems the one most admired – and hated. I've heard it variously described as 'a providential instrument for bringing the Gospel to a neo-pagan world' and 'the greatest menace to the Church since *Opus Dei*'.

So when I read that a speaker from 'Communione' was billed for this afternoon at *Pro Mundi Vita,* I hastened along to learn what I could from the horse's mouth. Unfortunately this particular quadruped seems to have shied, or strayed, or bolted, and my expectations were dashed: however, I'm told that the stable door remains open, so we may hope to be told all on another day.

In the meantime PMV did not fail to provide a very distinguished substitute speaker, who came along at short notice: Etienne Bisimwa from Zaire, Secretary-General of the International Catholic Students' Movement, who had addressed the Synod itself as an auditor. He is an extremely impressive young man and, if at all typical of his generation, the Church in Africa will not lack intellectual leadership. His subject was much the same as that of Monsignor Nicholls, and his analysis remarkably similar, though with a very different point of departure. He sees the Synod as *carrefour,* crossroads, and is, naturally, very sensitive to local-universal Church relationships and to processes of 'inculturation'.

He was particularly interesting on the *mokambi*, those lay pastors uniquely characterisic of the Church in Zaire, and who are truly *personae ecclesiae* to so many of the faithful there, except on the all too rare visits of a priest or bishop. They do their not inconsiderable best to maintain a fullness of church life – short of the all-important Eucharistic celebration. I asked him were they elected or appointed. Neither, he replied: rather do they 'emerge', following a lengthy and highly sophisticated process of consultation among all concerned. He emphasised that the process, and indeed the *mokambi* themselves are historically rooted in the pre-Christian religious culture of the people . . . A far cry from all this to the 'movements', about which Bisimwa's main reservation seems to be their essentially European character, which may or may not be suitable for export – although he could see how they respond to the need, in a secularised society, to 'create a space where one can talk about God'.

Listening to him, I couldn't help thinking of those days over a quarter of a century ago when the 'Belgian Congo' was one of the world's trouble-spots and, incidentally, one of the first opportunities for Irish soldiers to show their mettle as part of an international peace-keeping force. There were at the time no shortage of prophets of gloom and doom who saw nothing but darkness and savagery ahead, with the departure of 'Belgian civilisation' (Roger Casement might have a word to say on that). In the event, the new state of Zaire seems to have made as good a job of things as was done nearer home in the 1920s.

Someone suggested to me later that for Bisimwa to be critical of 'movements' was a little strange, since he is the chief executive of one which is internationally widespread. I take the point, and indeed it has helped to clarify my own inchoate feelings on the subject. Briefly, it seems to me that there are two kinds of movement in the Church. (And by 'movement' I mean any organisation or association whose size and/or dynamism make it a significant force nationally, e.g. the early Gaelic League, the 'Pioneers', or internationally – Anti-Apartheid, CND, Moral Re-Armament.)

My dichotomy is one of declared aim and scope. On the one hand we have had with us for some time, organisations like the St Vincent de Paul Society, the Young Christian Workers, Students, *Pax Christi*. They deserve to be called 'movements', but their 'area' of operation is limited, not by geography or jurisdiction, but from their very *raison d'être*. Each of them has a distinct job to do – one might even say a distinct ministry. On the other hand, *Opus Dei* and *Communione e Liberazione* seem to offer a total spirituality and indeed a total blueprint for apostolic action. And this is where I have a real difficulty, because it appears to me that they are duplicating, if not usurping, the role of the Church itself. I accept that they are utterly loyal to the Holy See, but their relationship with the local Church is more problematic – not just in matters of jurisdiction and authority, but in the 'focus' they seem to provide. And, if I'm right, it seems to me to represent a sad reversal of one of the great features of conciliar renewal . . . But maybe I'm quite wrong in this.

Friday 16th October

I often think that to call Rome the 'eternal city' is singularly inappropriate, since time and history are of its very pith and marrow. Ancient, medieval and modern; pagan, Christian and, maybe post-Christian; and all the styles and shapes of building and decorating that the changing culture of the centuries produced: Forum and Pantheon, small sturdy bridges and great *piazze,* basilicas and *palazzi,* and a maze of little streets and alleyways where butchers' shops and art galleries and vegetable stalls and tiny laundries and trendy boutiques and bars, and God knows how many restaurants and *trattorie,* share house-room with the apartments where the Romans (native and blow-ins) eat and drink and make love and fight and rear their children and live and die. The centuries live beside each other and on top of each other, and will, I believe and hope, go on doing so unless, and until, we blow the world up for the sake of the past or the future.

One place where the centuries do literally and spectacularly live on top of each other is the Basilica of San Clemente which is only a couple of hundred yards from the Colosseum and which has, since the seventeenth century, belonged to the Irish Dominicans. I enjoyed their hospitality today at luncheon.

It was just 130 years ago that the then Prior, Father Joseph Mullooly, set out on the remarkable adventure of discovery which revealed the layers of history that lie beneath what is now known to be the 'new' church, the twelfth-century basilica which is, to a large extent, a replica of the fourth-century one below. I'm not going to attempt even an outline account of the glories of either: there have been several scholarly works published on the subject since Fr

Mullooly, that inspired amateur, began to excavate, with the encouragement and guidance of his friend De Rossi who has been described as 'the father of archaeological science.'

Two points need, however, to be noted. One, that down below the fourth-century basilica itself, a third level of excavation revealed a temple of Mithras, god of a cult which flourished, especially among the Roman military in the early centuries of our era. (There is an area alongside it described as an early Christian *palazzo* but this is more problematic.) And, a remarkable link with Eastern Christianity exists in that the body of the great St Cyril, who with his brother Methodius not alone evangelised the Slavs but invented an alphabet for them, is buried in San Clemente. And that's another story still.

I hope my publisher won't accuse me of outrageous digression, going on like this. Too bad if he does: San Clemente is one of my enthusiasms. Anybody who visits Rome and doesn't follow the Mullooly trail doesn't deserve to go anywhere – and every Irish visitor should make it a top priority. And it was hinted to me today that all the secrets may not yet have been uncovered.

Saturday 17th October

I dropped into the Sala Stampa this morning on the off chance that the Pope might have left a message that he wanted me to ring him – or that a new Archbishop of Dublin had been named – or both. Nothing of the sort, I regret to say, but two of the familiar yellow Synod bulletins, each headed 'Summaries of the *in scriptis* Interventions'. These haven't of course come out of the working groups, but relate back to the plenary sessions that we thought we'd heard the last of. It appears that some of the Fathers may choose not to speak but to submit a written intervention – and, indeed, even those who do speak can expatiate in writing on their subject, at greater length than the eight minutes they are allowed *viva voce*. And so here we have further contributions from a patriarch, two cardinals, an archbishop, three bishops and the Father General of the Jesuits.

Maximos V. Hakim, Melchite Patriarch of Antioch, was one of the livelier voices of the Council. He can usually be expected to come up with something unusual.

This time he faults the use of the word 'lay' (as some others of us do!). His objection, it appears, is to the ambiguity of its French equivalent – *laic*, often meaning 'anti-clerical' or even 'anti-Christian'. And he points out that in Muslim countries, it suggests being 'against' the Koran, and God himself . . . A nice problem.

Cardinal Vidal from the Philippines, writes of what he calls 'popular religiosity', whose importance derives from the fact that 'the great majority of Christians . . . are not intellectuals . . . but simple folk with deep faith, but often little instruction'. He sees popular piety and religious practices as of great value, but stresses the need for 'vigorous promotion of *catechesis* and genuine inculturation . . .' along with 'attention to the *social dimension* and development of basic communities . . . and *ministries* entrusted to lay people – the only ones who may be of effective help'.

The Bishop of Uije in Angola, who is a Franciscan, refers to the condemnation of racial apartheid in the *Instrumentum Laboris*, but suggests that a religious apartheid also exists about which there is 'world-wide silence'.

> This happens in countries where there are racialist regimes, marxist ideologies. The faithful cannot become active Party members . . . have no voice in the political determination of their future, no access to government posts and, sometimes, no possibility of entering certain university faculties. When a citizen who is a believer wishes to join the Party in order to acquire these rights, or is invited to do so because of his qualities, he has to renounce the practice of his faith. This amounts to the same thing as racial apartheid, requiring a black person to become white in order to enjoy full civil rights . . .

He pointedly called on the international community to defend these millions of believers condemned to live as 'second-class citizens'.

Bishop Yves-Georges-René Ramousse, Apostolic Vicar of Phnom Penh, reminds us of one of the great tragedies of our time:

> In Cambodia there have been no Eucharistic celebrations since 1976. All the priests were killed during the Pol Pot revolution, and all the churches and other buildings either destroyed or confiscated. The laity themselves took charge of their communities. Their plea – that we don't forget about them because 'they cannot go on forever without the Eucharist'.

There are about half a million Cambodians living in diaspora.

250,000 of these have been able to find refuge in host countries where they now live. The rest are living in camps on the frontier of their own country and, except for a very few, do not even have refugee status. The normal conditions of these thousands of people is one of total dependence.

The number of Christian Cambodians living abroad is relatively few. Paradoxically, they experience great difficulty in finding that freedom and participation for which they had hoped. They have to overcome many obstacles so as not to give in to resignation and passivity. Given that there have been some happier experiences, a recent survey carried out among them reveals that considerable progress needs to be made with regard to the situation of the Cambodians in diaspora.

The service that the Church owes these members of the faithful is to welcome them with friendship and to do all she can to help them . . . They need to feel that the Church has confidence in them.

Fr Kolvenbach, the Jesuit General, touches on a matter in which his Society have been long and deeply involved: the 'educational mission of the Church', which is, he believes, afflicted at present by a 'vocational crisis'. He refers to 'internal doubts' as to whether Catholic educational institutions can have a 'prophetic function' today, but insists that they can indeed be 'bearers of the Spirit of the Lord' not least when 'other forms of dialogue and contact' are not possible. He goes on however:

There are grave doubts about an educational institution's capacity to serve the preferential option for the poor and the promotion of justice in the name of the Gospel . . . If it is true that the social teaching of the Church does not inspire all Catholic schools and colleges, this should not place in doubt their capacity – especially in universities – to form as followers of the Lord women and men who concretely incarnate the 'New Commandment'.

Sunday 18th October

Today is Mission, or rather *Missions* Sunday. I suppose that the plural 's' gives as a hint that the emphasis is still on 'foreign missions', even if we have all learned that mission, like charity, must begin at home – though neither should stay there – and that several of the younger churches may now send evangelists to those 'motherlands' which have themselves become *pays de mission*. Not that the 'pilgrim' impulse can ever be left out, whether at home or abroad.

'Go — make disciples of all nations' was the Pope's text this morning when he preached at the solemn liturgy in St Peter's for the canonisation of sixteen men and women martyred in, and near, Nagasaki in Japan 350 years ago. The first name among them is Lorenzo Ruiz, described by the Pope as 'husband and father of three children, who first collaborated with the Dominican Fathers in Manila and then shared their martyrdom': he is now the first canonised Filipino saint.

There were naturally huge numbers of pilgrims present from Asia, especially from the Philippines and Japan – as well as many from Spain, Italy and France where some of the sixteen were born. It was in a very real sense a Dominican occasion. As the Irish Master-General of the Order, Fr Damian Byrne, expressed it:

> These sixteen had the same desire as Saint Dominic to shed their blood for Christ. Some of them set out for Japan knowing they were already sentenced to death . . . Like St Dominic they trusted only in God's word. Bishop Salazar had learned in Mexico of the importance of not using the civil power to spread the Church. The Dominicans in the East were inspired by this example and they sought no favours from the civil authorities.

The history of the Church in certain other places might have been very different had their example been followed further afield!

That these canonisations should take place during the present Synod is highly appropriate, in view of the fact that five of the martyrs were lay people: Lorenzo Ruiz; two women, Magdalene of Nagasaki and Marina of Omura; a guide and interpreter (who had contracted leprosy), Lazaro of Kyoto; and a catechist, Michael Kurobioye.

'Representations of the catechists of all nations and continents' had, said the Pope, been invited to the ceremony. He greeted them as 'the ones who realise in large part, the missionary character of the Church', and he went on to say:

> Today the new saints speak to all who, urged by Christ's mandate . . . have gone throughout the world to proclaim the Good News

of salvation to all humanity, particularly to the most needy.

With their message and martyrdom they speak to catechists, to pastoral workers, to the laity, to all especially concerned with this Synod . . . They remind us that 'to die for the faith is a gift granted to few: but to live the faith is a call addressed to all' . . .

☆

Lunch with the Franciscans at San Isidoro where the Guardian Fr David introduced me to Bishop Wilfrid Fox Napier OFM of Kokstad, who, with Archbishop Naidoo of Capetown, represents the episcopal conference of South Africa – both are of the non-white majority. Bishop Fox and I discovered a common bond: we had both been students in Galway. He had been there, though, much later than I: I've noticed before that bishops are getting younger every year . . .

He talked freely about the situation in South Africa where, as he said, the bishops are now 'caught in the middle'. Bitterly resented by the government and their supporters for their stand on racial issues and their refusal to 'play the game', some more radical black leaders are disappointed with what they see as a half-hearted attitude to the 'people's struggle' – the issue here being, of course, the use of violence. A familiar problem, but one without easy answers.

Monday 19th October

Today, according to the Synod schedule, the working groups were due to report to the plenary session, with special reports from the auditors who were attached to the various groups. Following precedent, we all dutifully turned up in the Sala Stampa for a briefing on this morning's instalment. No briefing. This didn't mean that Diarmuid had gone on strike or decided to take a break in Capri – the same applied in all languages. No briefings this evening either. Alright, we'd make do with our bulletin summaries. No bulletins. By way of consolation prize, there will be another Grand Press Conference with star performers tomorrow, at which all will be revealed.

Correction. There were/are bulletins, but all they contain are the names of those who presented the twelve group reports (and, in the morning edition, those taking part in tomorrow's press conference.)

To the PMV centre this afternoon to hear Professor Alexandre Faivre of Strasbourg who is an authority on patristics and early christian history. His subject was dear to my heart: to put it in simple terms, a critical historical examination of the 'lay-cleric' dichotomy. His treatment of the question – on which he has written and published a great deal over the past three or four years (including an article, this year, in English, in *Lumen Vitae* XLII, 2) – was scholarly and cogent, if perhaps rather too detailed for an hour's talk, giving us little opportunity to digest his exposition of development in the periods surveyed. And it would be quite impossible for me to summarise it here. But I would suggest that what he had to say confirmed and expanded the biblical and historical evidence adduced by Seán Freyne and Werner Jeanrond in their essays in *Pobal*.

In his summing-up, Professor Faivre referred to Paul VI's *Motu Proprio* of August 1972, 'Ministeria Quaedam' which gave the first post-Conciliar encouragement to the institution of lay ministries. He notes that the Pope explicitly deprecated any blurring of the distinction between lay and clerical and he goes on:

> The Synod Fathers have the difficult task of identifying what may be expected from lay people within the framework of their mission and vocation. Will they now dare to ask how far their Christian liberty can extend? ? Will they go so far as to ask if they may call into question a distinction whose limitations are evident, while reserving their right to judge what may be opportune in concrete instances?

> To me it seems historically clear . . . that not only has the concept of 'lay persons' varied over the first centuries of the Church, but that there was a time when Christian communities lived without being aware of any 'clerical-lay' distinction . . .

As to the immediate implications, he quoted another historian 'of the contemporary period' Professor Giuseppe Albergo:

> It has become more and more clear over the past few years that the secular distinction of the Church as 'clergy' and 'laity' has entered a *terminal phase,* by reason of a crisis provoked not only by external pressures but also by its own internal contradictions. Both show the incurable inadequacy of the 'clergy-laity'

dichotomy as an expression of the profound reality of the Church which would correspond to the degree of ecclesial consciousness evoked by the Holy Spirit in our time.

Of course, as Faivre would be the first to admit, historical analysis and argument isn't everything, but we ignore it at our peril.

So where do we go from here? Well, I don't expect the Synod to change course and drop the dread dichotomy overboard. But there are hopeful signs . . .

Tuesday 20th October

The promised (or threatened) Press Conference took place after the end of this morning's plenary session of the Synod (of which more in a moment). The hall where it was held was packed, again including alleged journalists of doubtful provenance. It may be pure coincidence that a couple of hundred Americans 'from forty states' have arrived in town for a 'Gathering of Catholic Lay Leadership in Solidarity with the Synod' (of whom, also, more later).

The panel for the Conference consisted of Archbishop Henry d'Souza of Calcutta, Bishops from Nigeria and Honduras, and Ms Rivière, one of the auditors, who spoke in the Synod last week.

First we were given a run-down on the reports of the *circuli minores*. Since in the nature of things this was a synthesis, or series of syntheses, on what was said, it didn't really tell us very much about differences of approach, emphasis, even substance.

Some such differences *must* have been revealed in the actual reports, but the only one referred to (by Archbishop May) was on the matter of ordained and unordained ministries where we were told there was 'less unanimity' than on other questions, e.g. the parish, in regard to which there was (not surprisingly) a 'consensus' on its 'indispensability'. From the different areas of debate, what we were given were, as I've said, synthetic summations which tended to homogenise various shades of opinion – rather as happened to the consultation on the first *Lineamenta*, as published in the *Instrumentum Laboris* (see my Prologue above). I don't, of course, blame the five speakers, each of whom dealt with a different area: theology and ecclesiology; the 'movements'; parish and ministries; inculturation, women, young people; the laity and politics. What the commentators present clearly objected to and resented was that we were not allowed to do our own analysis (and perhaps synthesis) of what was said.

Blandness continued to rule during question-time. 'Safe' questions were welcomed and edifyingly commented on, e.g. 'Did the Fathers consider the plight of churches behind the Iron and Bamboo Curtains?' But more awkward queries were turned away with soft answers . . . Such performances are, I need hardly say, not peculiar to Vatican occasions: in the political world the Press Conference is recognised as one of the classic methods of concealing information – except, of course, when those in authority *want* to inform. Practised interrogators can of course often find out what they want to know by a combination of skill, skulduggery and persistence. Alas! Such voices were few and far between at today's event.

This morning's bulletin did unexpectedly provide material of interest, apart from the names of the auditors who reported from their groups. For the two bishops from Vietnam who have at last arrived were given the opportunity of making their formal 'interventions' – both well worth quoting.

The first to speak was Bishop Francis Xavier Nguyen Van Sang, Auxiliary of Ha Noi:

> The following are some of the characteristic traits of the South Vietnamese laity, since the time when the whole country fell under the communist regime.
>
> - After a period of confusion and anxiety, the faithful laity have been able to pull themselves together again and take courage. Enlightened by the teachings of the Second Vatican Council and the pastoral letter of the Vietnamese episcopal conference, they have found a way to 'live the Gospel in the heart of the nation'. They mix with their fellow citizens in the factory, school, hospitals, cooperatives, etc.
>
> - They have won the sympathy of all, even the atheist authorities, with their radiant charity, their honesty and their justice. The faithful laity are a presence there, even where there are no priests, no churches. They exercise the functions of the common priesthood of all the faithful by organising communities of prayer and charity, celebrating the liturgy of the Word of God and by bringing the sacraments to the sick.

Their role has been both useful and necessary because of the lack of priests.

- After the sixth general assembly of the Communist Party under the new leader, Mr Nguyên-Van-Linh, and as a result of the successful collaboration, in the field of economics, between the faithful laity and their atheist fellow citizens, the government has adopted an attitude of *détente* and openness towards religion. Two large seminaries have been opened and have admitted a number, albeit limited, of seminarians. New ordinations to the priesthood are permitted.

- The faithful laity both in the South and in the North have great devotion to the reception of the sacraments: above all, Holy Mass and Confession.

- An important question that engages our attention is the solid and profound formation of the faithful laity. What makes this work difficult is that the government has banned all movement and assembling together of christians. It has limited religious formation to that which is given in church during the space of one or two hours only on Sundays.

He was followed by Bishop Paul Marie Nguyen Minh Nhat, Coadjutor of Xuan Loc.

The christian lay person in Vietnam, proud of the faith of his forefathers, has found himself forced to affirm in his daily life his awareness that he belongs to the Church:

- By reception of the sacraments. In distant regions, the priests, who do manage to get there only seldom, soon become very tired because of the very many demands made upon them. Christians experience a very real need for the Eucharist. No distance discourages them from attending Mass, not even twenty to thirty, or at times, seventy kilometres. Every sort of transport is used (on foot, public transport, bicycles, even carts). Obstacles are usually overcome (tiredness, old age, rain). The Mass is understood as a coming together to pray to the Lord, who gives his Spirit and love, bringing a closer union between those who share this meal with the Pope, the Bishops and all those who work for the Church of God.

- The Vietnamese lay christian is unfamiliar with the texts of Vatican II. However . . . he has for a long time now been putting their essence into practice:

- By fulfilling . . . the duties of a good citizen in the work yards and the cooperatives where he is respected and holds posts of responsibility.

- In observing God's commandments, which results in less discord, fewer divorces, no abortion in the families, and few social problems: alcoholism, theft, corruption of morals.

- By enlisting in the army, to defend his country just like other citizens.

I don't know whether the two bishops would use the phrase 'bamboo curtain'. But the strength of their witness puts all our easy platitudes where they belong.

☆

The American invasion which I mentioned represents a formidable array of organisations – and acronyms. It's hosted by the National Association for Lay Ministry (NALM), the American Catholic Lay Network (ACLN) and the Pallottine Institute for Lay Leadership and Apostolate Research (PILLAR), and sponsors range from the National Office for Black Catholics, and the North American Conference for Separated/Divorced Catholics, to *Pax Christi,* USA. Each of the two hundred plus participants has paid something over 1,000 dollars – this includes air fare from New York, hotel, and some other perquisites. They actually came to town at the weekend but their first session (apart from liturgies) was last evening when 'a panel of experts' spoke on 'the Church and Society in Asia'. Unfortunately I was unable to attend, and I'll have to give this evening's session ('English-Speaking Countries') a miss also, as I'm bidden to sup at the General House of the Marists.

My invitation there, by the way, comes from their General Secretary, Fr Seán Fagan, whose nationality may be guessed at, and is one of the busiest men in Rome. There are quite a few Irishmen 'at the top' (or near it) of international religious bodies, old and new. The Augustinian General is Fr Martin Nolan, and Fr Damian Byrne is Master-General of the Dominicans – although he is quick to point out that he's only there by default: the first choice of the general chapter was Fr Albert Nolan [*sic*] of South Africa, who declined the honour, believing he should stay on the battle-ground. (Indeed he has been such a doughty fighter against apartheid and all its works, that, had he come to Rome, he might well have been prevented from returning.)

The actual superior general of the Marists is an Australian – his country and New Zealand are both strongly represented in the Society . . . So, I'm off to their establishment in the suburb of Monteverde. Tomorrow I'll report on an interesting session at *Pro Mundi Vita,* which actually links with the American Conference.

Wednesday 21st October

The Irish presence is coming back in some strength. A television team from RTE led by Billy FitzGerald is hard at work, and Nuala Kernan and Maureen Groarke (the great and good aforementioned from the Irish Laity Commission) have arrived as promised, along with two other lay women, from Armagh and Down and Connor.

Nuala, Maureen and I were in fact part of the ridiculously small audience who gathered at the PMV centre yesterday afternoon to hear two speakers from the US National Office for Black Catholics, Walter Hubbard of Seattle and Charles Hammock of Philadelphia. What they had to say was fascinating, and one listened with mixed feelings of shame, sadness, admiration and finally great hope.

The story of Black Catholic America is all too little known over here – and, I suspect, in White Catholic America too, or was, until recently. I summarise:

> There are approximately 1,295,000 Black Catholics in the United States of America. The Black Catholic population is about 5 per cent of the total Black population, 30,000,000, and approximately 3 per cent of the total Catholic population, 53,000,000, of the United States. The effects of evangelisation, together with the migration of Haitian Catholics to the United States, is evident in the increasing number of Black Catholics. Between 1975 and 1985, the number of Black Catholics increased by 42 per cent while there was only a 17.3 per cent increase in the overall Black population . . .
>
> However, this very growth also represents what is perhaps one of the greatest challenges to evangelisation currently facing the Church . . . Making its liturgy, style of worship, expression of its ancient truths relevant to a people, accustomed on the whole to a

non-Western European approach to God . . . represents an enormous task ahead for the American Church.

We believe there are vast potential and opportunities for evangelisation within the Black community. The Black community must take many steps to initiate action on our behalf; other action requires the cooperation and active encouragement of the entire American Church and World Church.

However, the social and economic condition of Black Americans creates particular obstacles to evangelisation efforts . . . The Black family is significantly poorer than the white family. In 1984, while 85 per cent of white children live with both parents, less than half of the Black children (44 per cent) live with both of their parents. Related to this is the distressing statistic that one out of every two children born of Black parents lives in poverty.

The US Bishops' letter on the US economy, *Economic Justice for All: Catholic Social Teaching and the US Economy* (1986), points out that Blacks are about three times more likely to be poor than whites. It is also widely reported that Black women have two and one-half times more abortions than white women . . .

There were about seven million Black Americans a century ago, and only an estimated one hundred thousand were Catholics. Most church leaders were not outspoken in their zeal for racial justice and Black evangelisation . . . In the South, Black Catholics studied in segregated schools and prayed in segregated churches, or had to sit in the galleries; Blacks received communion after whites and confessed sins in segregated confessionals . . .

During the 1920s and 1930s, Black candidates for the priesthood and religious life were generally not accepted into American seminaries and convents. Even today, there are diocesan seminaries that have graduated no more than two or three Black priests. The policies of the past explain why today there are fewer than 300 Black priests and less than 700 Black sisters. As late as 1959, five years after the 1954 US Supreme Court school desegregation ruling, *Jubilee* magazine could state that only two parochial schools were integrated out of 745 in the states of the South. Racism and resistance to integration were deeply rooted in history and culture.

Consequently, today Black Catholics often live a shadow existence in the larger Black community as well as in the larger

Catholic Church . . . The established 1.3 million Black Catholics in the country seem invisible in comparison to the great number of white Catholics. Black Catholics are seen as a negligible minority in the larger Black Christian community, and Black Catholics are seen as a negligible minority in the larger Catholic community. Unfortunately, some white Catholics look upon their Black brethren as a small group within the Church seeking more attention and influence than the numbers merit.

There have undoubtedly been considerable advances over the past thirty years, mainly achieved by Black Catholics themselves, inspired by the Civil Rights Movement. 'The inspiration of Dr Martin Luther King Jr, the struggle for justice, the building of Black pride, freedom, full equality were not just dreams – they became reality.' . . And, however belatedly, the American bishops threw their weight behind the struggle, fully acknowledging the Church's past participation in the 'sin of racism'. In a famous pastoral they wrote:

How great the scandal given by racist Catholics who would make the Body of Christ . . . a sign of racial oppression. Yet, all too often, the Church in our country has been for many a 'white church, a racist institution.'

And, as recently as last month, the Pope, speaking to Black Catholic leaders in New Orleans, spoke of 'the providential role' played by Martin Luther King in contributing to 'the rightful human betterment of Black Americans *and therefore to the improvement of American society as a whole.'*

There are few Black bishops in the American church – one diocesan ordinary and, I think, nine auxiliaries. And the NOBC report pays tribute to Black priests, sisters, brothers and deacons who have been 'very important to the history and growth of the Black community'. However . . .

It is apparent that in the near future we are not likely to experience any radical increase in the number of vocations. Thus the future of the Church in the Black community rests in a special way with the laity . . . Evangelisation now becomes more and more the province of lay Catholics.

And the report insists on the need for training (including leadership training) for this task.

We asked whether US Irish Catholic attitudes had improved.

Walter Hubbard's gentle and kindly answer seemed to add up to 'yes – but not much' . . . Is the Church now seen by Blacks to be the 'Church of the Poor'? Well, again, yes – to some extent. Maureen Groarke said her experience in the States some years ago was that the people who cared most about Black poverty were Jews . . . They agreed.

After lunch today (at the Irish College), I had to deal with some urgent personal business which got in the way of my attendance at fringe events. But I have plenty to think about: my encounter with the Black Americans has affected me far more deeply than I might have imagined. After all, we have heard equally moving witness from other voices, especially from the Second and Third Worlds. On reflection, I think two factors have made this one special.

First of all there's the personal element. The two speakers spoke to us close-up: the accident of there being a very small audience at the PMV made it all very intimate. And secondly, the very fact of their coming from a world which is historically and culturally close to us made what they said all the more, literally, shocking. It was 'our kind of people' who did these things to their fellow-Catholics: who put them in segregated churches, or made them sit on their own in a gallery, and made them tell their sins in a separate 'box' and brought them Christ's Body only when *we* were fed . . . And we talk so easily of reconciliation!

Thursday 22nd October

Up at the crack of dawn – well, a little later actually – in order to be at the Jesuit Curia by nine o'clock for what is described as 'an American think-tank' on 'The Laity and the Church.' And these Americans are addicted to the vice of punctuality – which shows how marginal Irish and Italian influence must be after all.

As I approached the building on the corner of Borgo Santo Spirito and Via dei Penitentieri (very close to the Vatican), there was a bit of a breeze, reminding me that this, they say, is the windiest corner in Rome. And, of course, the Romans will tell you why.

It appears (or so they say) that, once upon a time, the Devil and the Wind went for a walk. As they were passing the Jesuit HQ the Devil said:

'I've just remembered I've something to discuss with Father General. Will you wait a moment?'

And the Wind (or so they say) is still waiting.

The principal speaker at the 'think-tank' is Ms Sally Cunneen. She, and Joe, her husband, who is also here, started the American radical Catholic journal *Cross-Currents* in the early fifties: it is happily still going strong. Her talk is entitled: 'Women's Issues – Church/World Issues' and, as I listen, there's hardly a paragraph, a sentence that doesn't make me want to say: 'Yes, yes, yes!, I *must* get her to agree to have it published in Ireland by Austin Flannery in *Doctrine and Life!*: he doesn't know it yet, but he will. So I'm not going to try to summarise her paper here, or even to quote extensively from it. But I will quote from two of her earlier paragraphs, which I think spell out her thesis that *'women's issues are in reality both church and world issues'*.

> I want to begin by recalling that it was John XXIII who first pointed out, in *Pacem in Terris* . . . that one of the key signs of contemporary life was the awakening desire of women for free and responsible participation in determining their own lives 'in the social and economic sphere, in the fields of learning and culture, and in public life.
>
> I want to dwell on John's words for they are truly prophetic, issued in the very year Betty Friedan's book appeared. This elderly Italian pope already knew that, if women did not rethink and reshape their own roles, neither the church nor the world could carry out the common task the Spirit called them to: 'The task of restoring the relation of the human family in truth, justice, love and in freedom' . . . His was not the severely rational, bureaucratic mind that divides reality into sacred and secular, or assigns priests to the care of 'souls', women to the care of children, and men to the care of the body politic . . .

When Sally Cunneen finished speaking – and was given a standing ovation – the rest was silence. I mean to me.

There were several other speakers but I can't remember a word of what they said, except for one wonderful woman who articulated two of my own deepest antipathies. She said she 'cringes' when she hears the word *formation* . . . and also when she hears people (especially Catholics) say: 'We have the truth'. Truth, as she so rightly added, is not something you possess – it's something you never stop searching for. I would only add that happiness is when

94

truth possesses *us* . . . As to 'formation', I know it's used quite innocently and with good intention, but we should never, never talk about 'forming' anybody. Only God can do that. In fact he has.

Anyway, what's wrong with 'education'?

Over in the Sala Stampa the recently deserted halls are buzzing with a swarm of hacks, some of whom I recognise but others are oddly unfamiliar. What are they doing? Do they – dreadful thought – know something I don't? Thank God for national solidarity!

Paddy Agnew, the only Irish journalist at present resident in Rome, puts me out of my agony. This, he kindly explains, has nothing to do with the Synod: the whole press corps, native and foreign, have been alerted by the word that a statement on Vatican Finances is to be issued at any moment. At long last, all will be revealed! Not being a 'Vaticanologist', and still less an authority on finance, the information didn't really stir my blood. However, I stood by with the rest, till Paddy, with Ulster good sense, decided nothing was to be gained by hanging around since the agencies would have the story anyway, and comment, if any, could wait. So he took me off to lunch at the Foreign Press Club.

Back to the Americans this evening for a 'Panel on South America'. It was as dull and disappointing as this morning's session was exhilarating. None of the panellists displayed any particular expertise, although they all had, in some way, Latin-American backgrounds, and while I was there (I had to leave shortly before the end) nobody came to grips with any of the questions that such a subject should provoke.

I spotted Gary Mac Eoin in the audience and wondered why he for one wasn't included in the panel in view of his being a recognised authority on Latin-American affairs generally, and the religious dimension in particular. He has been writing on the subject for some years and continues to contribute reports and comments to the *National Catholic Reporter* and other journals. His exclusion cannot have been due to national prejudice since Nuala Kernan, and a Canadian lay woman, were asked to join the panel and to speak on 'their own countries' – whatever that had to do with the subject.

There was a curious ambivalence of approach, or rather, as it seemed, a confusion between two very distinct though related issues: the 'Hispanic' element in United States Catholicism, and the Church in Latin America itself. (Clearly 'South' America was a misnomer, as there were frequent references to Central America.)

Neither issue was discussed in any depth, or with any great sense of urgency. Having heard the Black story, the situation of the new 'Hispanics' cried out for informed, sensitive treatment with an awareness of the complex social and cultural aspects involved. What we heard were mostly pious generalities . . . The second issue got equally superficial treatment with a degree of what I can only describe as pussy-footing. Nobody seemed to know or care that Christians are suffering in Latin America today under regimes which are supported, not to say propped up, by the United States taxpayer.

Friday 23rd October

Bright and early to the Sala Stampa where copies of the press release on 'Vatican Finances' were waiting, crisp and fresh. Well, fairly fresh: the document was in fact issued late yesterday afternoon. I hadn't intended to comment on it here, as it's not particularly relevant to the Synod. However I think two aspects of its content are worth a thought.

I should say first of all that there are no dreadful revelations. It comes as no surprise that the Holy See is in the red, and looks like staying there for some time. In 1987, total income is expected to be just under 70 billion lire (about IR£38 million) with expenses amounting to over *twice* that amount. In other words the deficit will be around IR£40 million. It is however noted that this will be under one per cent more than last year: there have been some generous contributions, as well as 'strict' budgetary controls.

The stated purpose of the press release is to announce that the 'Council of Cardinals for the Study of the Organisation and Economic Problems of the Holy See' has approved a letter to be sent next month 'to the bishops of the world expressing thanks for increased generosity' and asking for more of the same. The Secretary of State, Cardinal Casaroli, presided at a meeting of the Council held earlier this week and he is quoted as saying that

> . . . the income of the Holy see comes largely from investments made from funds paid by the Italian government in 1929 in compensation for properties taken from the Church during the

reunification of Italy. Since the increase in the number of central services offered by the Church in response to the Second Vatican Council, he noted that the traditional sources were no longer adequate to maintain the services offered by the Holy See to the Church throughout the world and expressed the hope that the bishops, religious communities and faithful throughout the world who benefited from these services might be more generous in supporting them.

In recent years, deficits have been covered by the free-will offerings of the faithful made to the Holy Father and by operating reserves. Such operating reserves have now been almost completely exhausted and offerings from all around the world are still far from sufficient to cover the expenses of the services provided.

The first point to be made is the obvious one that it is no longer good enough to issue bland statements in the name of a 'Council of Cardinals' on such a serious matter, involving the whole Church and, at the paying end, especially the laity. If ever there was a practical example of the need for de-clericalisation surely this is it. Nobody, of course, would suggest that the Pope's senior advisers should not have a leading role in this area, as elsewhere, but surely what is glaringly obvious is the need for lay collaboration – including that of financial and administrative experts – in tackling what must be seen as a potential, if not an actual, source of scandal. And, to begin with, details of the 'central services' provided should, as a matter of urgency, be published in plain language. Without this it will be increasingly difficult to maintain contributions at the present level, let alone raising that level.

There has been already far too much speculation, informed and otherwise, as well as plain rumour and gossip, arising out of the Banco Ambrosiano affair, and the role of Archbishop Marcinkus. As I have said at tedious length already, the only antidote to this sort of thing is to publish the facts.

It can't be denied that at parish level most of us are still living in the past as far as realistic 'support for our pastors' is concerned. Even those of us who know only too well what overheads mean, at home or at work, seem to think that the Church is miraculously unaffected by such nasty things as price-rises and inflation. Many good Catholics still give less per week than they do, say, for a week's newspapers – or a single round of drinks. Two often it's still the have-nots who give with a generosity far beyond their means.

But. People have a right to know what they are giving *for*. This information is now often reasonably available at local level, so why not from Rome?

There is however another side to the whole question, one touching on that local-universal relationship which is the context in which so much of the Synod agenda must be seen. Cardinal Casaroli cites the Second Vatican Council as causing an 'increase in the number of central services offered by the Church'. I'm sure he's right, though I cannot call many examples to mind. On the other hand the Council did emphasise the *autonomy* (though not of course the *sovereignty*) of the local Church, and many of us looked forward – and still do – to much growth and benefit for God's people as a fruit of this insight. In many parts of the world, indeed, these expectations have been and continue to be realised, not least in places where poverty and oppression have evoked a response which can only be seen as the work of the Holy Spirit. It would be a tragedy if this kind of growth and pastoral action, rooted in peoples of many cultures and circumstances, were to weaken or fade.

I know I am not alone in fearing such a possibility, due to a clouding of the vision of *Lumen Gentium* and what some have gone so far as to describe as a new centralism – and indeed 'a new Pelagianism'. This latter accusation may well be an exaggeration, but centralising signs and tendencies are by no means absent. One recognises of course that those responsible are moved by zeal, and by a sense of universal mission which, though genuine, is I believe mistakenly directed. I'll be returning to this topic in another connection, but I see the problem of finance as very much part of the pattern.

For the moment, let me just relate what the very distinguished head of a world-wide and long established Society said to me the other evening (before the press release was issued). He believes that the Vatican's financial problems are providential: that they are a real 'sign of the times', an indication that our present 'top-heavy' system can't survive and that devolution, decentralisation – call it what you will – is inevitable. And he sees it as a positive challenge to new thinking in the Church.

This afternoon, before he attended the evening session of his working group, Fr John Vaughn, Minister-General of the Friars

Minor, spared a little time to talk to me about a matter which I've already referred to (in the Prologue to this volume). Fr John is an American and he was accompanied by an Irish member of his Council, Fr Louis Brennan.

The matter in question relates to the 'status' of the order – is it clerical, or lay or both or neither? The detail is more complex than might appear from reports by which my own interest was aroused, but the central issue is ultimately simple. The Vatican authorities cannot accept the 'mixed' status which the friars claim, on both historical and theological grounds, but the question may still be regarded as open to further study, and Fr John and his associates hope it can be resolved as they see it. (On a practical level, it involves the right of unordained friars to hold any office in the order, without special permission.)

While it is, of course, very much a domestic question for the friars, its implications and possible repercussions could spread very wide. Francis did not see himself as a cleric when he gathered his first community, and was still a layman, it appears, when the Pope confirmed their rule. He was later ordained a deacon, and others of the community were priests, but he did not see those as constituting a ruling class. And in fact his successor Brother Elias was himself a lay member when he became leader of the community.

I know that other orders and congregations have been thinking on similar lines to the friars, and while one can't foresee the outcome, it looks as if 'a third force' neither lay nor clerical may develop in the Church: I refer of course to canonical status. This could be a development of considerable significance for what I see as the ultimately inevitable declericalisation of ministry – ordained as well as unordained.

☆

A bulletin issued this afternoon reports that, at the morning session, a first outline text of *Propositions*, collated by the special secretary and the reporters from the working groups, was presented to the Synod. The paragraph which followed may clarify the procedure – or then again it may not:

> In an attempt to unify as much as possible the various themes under discussion, without at the same time omitting any significant contribution, the formulation of Propositions was

preceded in each group by a collation and synthesis of ideas. This attempt, in itself principally a technical exercise, will provide the groups (who meet this afternoon and tomorrow) with a single text. Their task will be ultimately to draw up proposals to be submitted to the Holy Father.

Tomorrow afternoon the *relator*, the special secretary and the group reporters will draw up an *elenchus definitivus* – a definite list of proposals to be submitted for the Synod's approval.

We are also informed that 'a first draft of the Message of the Synod to the People of God' was presented this morning by Bishop Castrillón Hoyas of Colombia (Memo: find out why he?)

Saturday 24th October

Does anyone remember a cartoon-advertisement that used to appear every weekend in one of the Irish daily papers based on the phrase 'This is Saturday'?: the idea being that once you realised that the shops would be closed next day, you rushed out to stock up on the brand of sweets in the ad. I take it that in Italy today you go out early to the news-stand to make sure of your copy of *Il Sabato*, a journal now in its tenth year, published in Milan, appearing every Saturday, and selling for the equivalent of one Irish pound. Very well produced in tabloid form, with excellent lay out and illustrations (mostly black and white, but some in colour), it runs to forty pages and does well on ads.

Today's edition has Cardinal Ratzinger on its front page, smiling a knowing smile: inside, we are told, we can read a long 'conversation' which *Sabato* journalists had recently with him, 'touching on the most crucial aspects of Catholic life today'.

There are substantial articles on political and social affairs, at home and abroad. There are features on science, ecology, the arts, books, theatre, television, the cinema, motoring. What is different is the 'angle', the point of view, the approach. For *Il Sabato* is not just a 'Catholic' weekly, it is the voice of *Communione e Liberazione* . . . Well, one of its voices. For its monthly publication, *30 Giorni* [Thirty Days] is equally well-produced, even more glossy and sophisticated in its well-heeled way: clearly there's no lack of money. It appears simultaneously in Spanish, French and Portuguese, as well as Italian, with separate Spanish editions for Spain and Mexico. I await the English edition with interest.

Again, the text is as professional as the lay out, and, yet again, the 'movement' rules OK. The October edition naturally features the Synod, with 'close-up' views of personalities and issues. A commentator in the influential and highly readable Rome daily *La Repubblica* remarks that if *30 Giorni's* 'politicisation' of the story appeared in a secular 'journal' there would be an outcry on the grounds that the writer failed to recognise that the Church (and accordingly the Synod) is mystery!

One of *Communione e Liberazione's* main targets seems to be the American Bishops' Conference, or at least their spokesmen, both here and during the Pope's visit to the States. As well as direct sniping (especially at Cardinal Bernardin and Archbishop Weakland) by their own hacks, *30 Giorni* features a rather smarmy interview with Jean-Loup Dherse (remember, Mr Channel Tunnel?) in the course of which he is quoted as expressing admiration for papal and Vatican statements on socio-economic issues, but describing the US bishops' pastoral on the same subject as 'a deliciously American exercise'. I will not quote him further, as I suspect that some of the interview may be libellous. But when I read what this former Vice-President of the World Bank – who seems to have had a charismatic conversion experience – is purported to have said, I can only recall a famous remark made in another context: 'Well he would, wouldn't he?'

Both *Sabato* and *30 Giorni,* it is only fair to say, do, from time to time, publish useful and well-informed articles on public issues. But neither has a reputation for excessive charity when dealing with those of whom they disapprove, especially within the Church . . . My own overall reaction is rather like that of the great Duke of Wellington, when presented with some new recruits: 'I don't know if they'll frighten the enemy, but by God they frighten me!' . . .

Sunday 25th October

This morning the Pope performed the final canonisation of the Synod period, and once again the newly declared saint was a layman. Giuseppe Moscati was a doctor from Benevento, a graduate of

Naples medical school and a distinguished physiologist. He died in 1927 at the age of forty-seven, having worked 'with extraordinary intensity' on all levels of his profession. In his homily, the Pope said:

> By nature and vocation, Moscati was first and foremost *a doctor who heals:* response to the needs of men and to their sufferings was for him a pressing demand which could not be denied . . . The human warmth with which he visited the sick – especially the most poor and abandoned – was such that people sought him out. He was a forerunner and protagonist of the humanisation of medicine . . . In his own words: 'Not science but love has transformed the world; only a very few have made history through science; but all can be signs of life everlasting, in which death is only a stage, if they dedicate themselves to the good.'

☆

The Synod, and all of us whom it has brought to Rome, have been very fortunate in that at least it has been a remarkably fine October. There was some thunder and lightning early on, accompanied by the kind of rain that makes the worst we get in Ireland merely a 'soft day, thank God'. But it all passed over very quickly and these autumn days and evenings have been like a good Irish summer.

So when I was invited to get away from it all – I mean the Synod and all its works – and get out of Rome for a few hours today, I jumped at the chance. Friends (Tony is Irish, Julia English) are reluctantly moving out of their tiny flat in Trastevere, and they took me to see their new place in Trevignano, about forty kilometres north west of Rome. It's a charming little lake-side town, and even though there were a lot of Romans there for the day, and it attracts many visitors, it has kept its character – and its 'characters'. At least, that's what the tourists would call them.

I mean the semi-circle of men in their Sunday suits, sitting outside the café, not drinking (though one was eating a bun), not playing cards, and hardly talking. Sitting and thinking. Or maybe just sitting. But looking at those stern Etruscan faces, not so much carved as broken from stone, I knew this was a parliament to be treated with respect. A sort of Synod. Quieter, but perhaps wiser.

They did turn their heads a little when a christening party passed on their way to the church (whose electric *campanile* played the Lourdes hymn every quarter-hour on the quarter-hour – or maybe it only sounded like that). This being Italy, the child was robed like a prince.

And later into the *Postiglione,* an old coaching-inn on the Via Casia, outpouring from another church, came a wedding party this time, to eat and drink and celebrate. Need I say that the bride outshone the shining shimmering afternoon? – and I don't mean the shimmer effect of all those litres of *vino bianco.*

In the rites of passage, sacred and secular are still as one.

Monday 26th October

The definitive list of Synod proposals which were to have been drawn up over the weekend are due for presentation and discussion this morning. However not a word is being allowed to trickle out till tomorrow when amendments will, it appears, be taken (based on the thinking to be done this afternoon by the Fathers 'at home'. In a more worldly assembly this would be the time for alliances, lobbying, horse-trading and backstairs intrigue. Not having the resources of *30 Giorni* I won't speculate).

Pro Mundi Vita have really been doing a great job in bringing us voices from all over the world. This afternoon we hear from Sri Lanka in the person of Father S.J. Emmanuel, Rector of St Francis Xavier Seminary in Jaffna, who despite his initials and his job is not a Jesuit. He has been acting as a theological advisor to the Federation of Asian Bishops' Conferences and addressed their assembly in Tokyo last month. In the unhappy conflict between the Singhalese majority and the Tamil minority in the north, he makes no secret of his loyalty: within the minority (mainly Hindu), he represents a smaller christian minority.

He is severely critical of the Church, the majority of whose bishops are Singhalese, for its 'Red Cross' behaviour – burying the dead and caring for the wounded – instead of assuming its 'due prophetic role of evaluating and reacting to the human situation of suffering and oppression'. He concedes that, belatedly, the bishops expressed their concern in a pastoral letter, issued three years ago, but that it did not carry 'a hard-hitting message to those responsible for evil'. He attributes this over-cautious attitude to an old fear among Singhalese Catholics, once accused of colonialism: they feel now is the time to prove their patriotism, in order to 'ensure a safe future' at the expense of suppressing their 'concern for justice and solidarity with the distant suffering'.

One would like to hear another side of the story, but Fr Emmanuel's sincerity and authority cannot be gainsaid. And his dilemma about violence is, he says, that of 'the church of the minority' who can only 'condemn terrorism in general but not act concretely against the militants' without whom the people say they would have been 'wiped out long ago' by undisciplined state forces . . . A not unfamiliar tale.

Another very different part of the Third World, but one also where it is easier to generalise about violence than to deal with the concrete situation, is Colombia (not the Sri Lankan capital but the South American state). At an earlier PMV session, Hector A. Torres, a journalist from Bogota, editor of the review *Solidarided,* which is published by a group of basic communities and other christians, provided some chilling statistics on the violation of all human rights in that country. To the question 'Who are responsible for the campaign of terror?' his reply was unhesitant and unambiguous: the army, the wealthy classes, and 140 'death squads' whose existence has been officially confirmed by the government, and who are being openly armed from the official arsenal. It is, he says, a war designed to crush finally the struggle for the land – especially that of the 'Indians whose claim to their ancient patrimony is theoretically conceded '- as well as to prevent the development of genuine trade unions, and of a progressive political party which would break the present tweedledum-tweedledee duopoly of alternating liberal and conservative governments. The campaign has resulted in political assassinations, disappearances, torture and widespread repression.

The facts and figures quoted by Torres reveal a situation which, literally, cries to heaven for vengeance, and surely has a claim on the active concern of christians everywhere. But he indicated that the attitude of most of the bishops in Colombia is, to put it mildly, ambiguous. Here again is an example of the plain people of God living their faith in a situation of appalling injustice, and doing so for the most part with little leadership from on high.

And what can *we* do? I mean people like you and me in Ireland and elsewhere in the lands of comparative justice and comparative affluence. Some of you are doing quite a bit – Franciscans and Columbans, and young men and women going out at their own expense to help the Nicaraguans to save the coffee crop, and all the other good things that our sisters and brothers are doing for their sisters and brothers . . . But it's not nearly enough. Now that our rulers have decided (on our behalf) to cut development aid, we need to do more and more in other ways . . . (Memo: what the hell can or will *I* do?)

One of the most puzzling aspects of this Synod has been the ecumenical dimension. Like the dog that *didn't* bark in the night. On this of all subjects, surely the witness and experience of other christians would have been invaluable: but, not alone was there no provision made for this, but it wasn't even mentioned in the *Lineamenta*, the *Instrumentum Laboris*, or as far as I am aware, in any of the interventions in plenary session. The only indirect reference made to the laity, in either theology or praxis, outside of the Latin tradition, was in the interventions of some of the speakers from eastern churches (within the Roman communion). It might have been imagined that, over twenty years after the Vatican II decree on ecumenism, and, indeed, in the light of all the interchurch dialogue that has been going on, not alone with the 'dissident' churches of the east, but also (and this has been equally if not more important) with those of the post-Reformation tradition, that it would have been impossible *not* to invite representatives of some of these churches to speak to the Synod. The fact that this didn't happen is a rather disturbing indication of the superficiality of our ecumenical awareness.

Those of us who remember the remarkable contribution made by the observers at Vatican II may well be saddened at what must be regarded as a valuable opportunity stupidly missed. I was reminded of this at dinner this evening, with one of the pioneers of the Secretariat of Christian Unity, John Long, an American Jesuit, who is now vice-rector of the Pontifical Oriental Institute, and a distinguished ecumenical theologian, specialising in the orthodox and other eastern traditions.

I learned a great deal from him about the complex history of the lay-clerical situation in the Greek and Russian churches. As in the west, imperial politics and the establishment of christianity played a crucial role, as did, at a later stage, the long Turkish hegemony in the near east, and in Europe itself. And I was particularly interested in his account of the way theology, as a professional academic discipline, has become almost a lay preserve. (I recalled an afternoon in Zagorsk when I had a long conversation with two Russian orthodox theologians, both of them laymen. They were very open and pleasant, but also very conservative indeed. I remember asking them was there any move to bring the modern Russian vernacular into the liturgy instead of Old Slavonic: they said that 'the people wouldn't like it'!)

But, of course, to us in Ireland and in the west generally, the Protestant and Anglican traditions are of more immediate relevance. In the Church of Ireland the laity play an important part in government and administration, at parish and diocesan level, but also in the national synod. Among the Presbyterians 'lay power' seems more evident still, not always with benevolent effect – as more than one ecumenically minded minister in the north has learned very painfully. But it is precisely the fact that the situation both east and west is very varied, and by no means as simple as some Catholic radicals would like to believe, that it would have been immensely helpful to the Synod to have been given informed and balanced accounts of what goes on. And on the theological and ecclesiological levels too there could be much to learn. The ordination of women in the Presbyterian church is now fully accepted, if not yet widespread, in Ireland, while women are being admitted to the ordained diaconate in the Church of Ireland: their admission to the priesthood is unlikely to be long delayed, as elsewhere in the Anglican communion. It is ironic that 'ecumenical' arguments have been adduced in that communion *against* ordination!

Tuesday 27th October

Black Tuesday

Well, what would you call it, if you were a newspaper reporter ready to send home the first fruits of the long incubation period which has been going on since the Synod Fathers broke up into their working groups nearly a fortnight ago – and now you're told that the only news is that there's no news? That it has been decided not to release any details of the proposals which have been submitted by the different groups and have now been collected and put into a definite list on which this morning *modi,* (amendments) were to be offered.

And that even when the process is completed, the final vote taken (on Thursday morning), and the final version of the proposals incorporated into the synodal document which will be submitted to the Pope – even then, we have as now no guarantee that any information as to the content of the document will be published.

I've never seen so many flabbergasted journalists in one place at the same time. Maybe we shouldn't have been. Most of us are all too well aware that when it comes to communicating with the media the Vatican runs the Kremlin a close second. But hope keeps putting up a brave fight against experience and, as today, it continues to go down fighting.

Since I've no incredulous news editor waiting at the other end of a phone line, or watching for telefax or whatever, I'm not as directly affected as are many of my colleagues. But I can sympathise with them – I can remember holes of fifteen or thirty minutes waiting to be filled on a radio schedule in the early days of the Council, and the desperate attempts to find material and beat the deadline. It's the sort of thing you look back on years later with a nostalgic glow, but it is not, as they say, funny at the time. Not at all funny.

But of course to regard the whole thing as a battle of wits between the Synod authorities and the media is to connive in a fiction which only trivialises a very serious matter. For, like it or not, in a democratic or pseudo-democratic society the 'media' are precisely that: the *means* of communicating with the great mass of the people. To keep information from the press, the radio, the television reporters, is to keep it from the ordinary citizen who has no other, privileged, access to what is, in theory, a matter of public concern and therefore public knowledge.

If that's the case in civil society why or how can it be any different in the Church? Or are all the fine and noble words about the people of God in the documents of Vatican II just that: fine and noble, but empty and meaningless? And isn't it particularly ironic that this 'blackout', this decision to keep the people in the dark, this paper wall erected around the sanctuary of secrecy, should come from a Synod which was called to celebrate the dignity of the ordinary Christian?

Ironic, and more than a little sick. Of course, within an hour of the announcement (made by an embarrassed and stonewalling Diarmuid Martin), the forbidden information became available – for the price of a photocopy. Or rather two photocopies: one of the first collection of some sixty proposals, as they emerged from the *circuli minores*, and one of the second, edited, collation in which the proposals – now reduced to fifty-four – are presented for voting and amendment.

This second text will have been through the mill this morning (I gather the amendments run into several hundreds), and will be replaced by a third and final *elenchus* to be voted on, on Thursday. So I will spare you any comparison of marks 1 and 2, except to note an apparently significant discrepancy between them.

Proposal 4a (in text 1) suggests that 'ecclesiastical offices – liturgical, included – which may be exercised without holy orders should be open also to women and girls as appropriate'. This has disappeared without trace from text 2 . . . I look forward to text 3.

So the 'blackout' has proved, not just bad, but mad. The blinds are pulled down but they turn out to be transparent. Or nearly so. In fact, this last situation is much worse than the first from everyone's point of view. It has simply meant more work for the journalists, and, since the texts are in Latin, their reports may in many cases leave much to be desired in the way of accuracy. And if there are any serious misstatements, the blame must rest squarely with the Synod secretariat. An authorised translation, officially available, would have made amateur 'versions' unnecessary, and so helped to avoid that 'misrepresentation by the media' of which all institutions love to complain. And while I should be the last to pretend that media people always do their job well, the one way of ensuring that they'll do it badly is the kind of mindless behaviour that we were exposed to today . . . Who was responsible? Well, no doubt we'll soon be told – on all sides.

This afternoon the admirable Jerzy Turowicz talked to an overflow audience at *Pro Mundi Vita*. I missed most of it, as I had to do a piece for BBC Belfast. But clearly, Jerzy, speaking both in French and in English, gave his usual balanced view of things as they really are in Poland, and how the laity there serve the church in their unique world.

I recalled a visit in 1977 when the present Pope was still archbishop of Cracow. It was Corpus Christi and the great folk festival surrounding the traditional procession was in full swing. No one could believe that the regime was antagonistic to religion – or to freedom of expression. But they were, and only the determination of a united people could win what gains they could, like the new church at Nova Huta which after many refusals and obstructions rose to serve a new community industrialised and removed from its traditional roots.

I asked Jerzy about similar communities in the continuing transformation of agricultural Poland into an industrial nation. (Farming is now a minority occupation.) He was able to report that several new churches had been and are being built, but that there is still a shortage: in the meantime, people meet elsewhere in liturgical assembly, often breaking the law to do so.

Back to the Sala Stampa for another briefing. This time at least we learned a little of what was going on, e.g. the voting for the new *concilium* or council of the Synod, the body which maintains continuity from year to year. And there was some speculation on what the next Synod might discuss: faith and culture; youth; a further investigation of previous synodal topics.

As to the real matter in hand, it appears the proposals are being reconsidered in the light of the amendments, which are said now to number nearly 800. We must wait and see.

Wednesday 28th October

Breakfast this morning consists of *caffè latte* and a bun in the excellent and inexpensive bar of the 'Greg' – the Gregorian University, one of Rome's two chief Catholic academies: the other being the Angelicum. They have both gradually moved from being deeply conservative institutions to a position where scholars, like Liam Walsh OP, can hold a chair (in the Angelicum), and the Australian Gerald O'Collins can become dean of theology (in the Gregorian).

It was an appointment with O'Collins that brought me so early there. He is as unpompous and lively-minded as when I first met him on the printed page, writing with courageous clarity of insight on the virgin conception and the resurrection of Jesus – and always with radical biblical orthodoxy. He is now devoting a considerable proportion of his time to administration, a necessary evil, it seems, if we are not to let the bureaucrats take over. He has all the air of a man who is happily 'stretched'.

On the Synod, his expectations are not high but he takes the view that as an institution, or rather as a process, it is of considerable value

– with all its limitations. It does preserve the idea of 'collegiality in action' which was one of the insights of the council and is exceedingly important just now, when there might appear to be a certain centralising tendency gaining ground.

His remarks were, in a way – a very different way – echoed this afternoon by Peter Hebblethwaite when he gave the final talk of the session to *Pro Mundi Vita*. Pessimistic as to the outcome of the month's deliberations, he felt that *effective* collegiality was pretty well a dead duck (my phrase, not his) and that the central authority was determined to keep it so. But what is sometimes called *affective* collegiality – the experience, perhaps the dynamic, of coming together and working together in however constrained a way – continues to maintain a sense of fellowship among local bishops from all corners of the world . . . As ever, Hebblethwaite's talk as a whole was shrewd, well-informed, and rooted in a deep (if unbiddable) commitment.

Another English voice this afternoon – this time from within the Synod – Patricia Jones, who is a full-time pastoral and administrative worker in the Archdiocese of Liverpool, and one of the auditors: you'll remember that she spoke at one of the early synodal sessions. She is very emphatically glad to have been there, and to have taken part in what she sees as a very substantial move forward towards bringing 'us' and 'them' together.

By no means uncritical of the process in detail, she is convinced that it nevertheless is of enormous value as a living sign of the living Church – ordained and unordained. She spoke with particular enthusiasm of her experience of the small groups, the *circuli minores,* where her presence as a laywoman was gradually taken for granted – and not alone her presence, but her full participation in what was said and done. She is firmly of the opinion that such practical initiatives at all levels are pointers to the way forward. After all, pastoral councils and basic communities are now taken for granted – and these are obviously dependent on the cooperation of cleric, religious, laymen and laywomen. *Praxis* will, she believes, lead eventually to acceptance of principle.

I nearly forgot to mention today's 'news' as issued at briefings and in bulletins. Nothing substantial. Voting for the Synod council still goes on (the first ballot failed to produce a result), and the 'heads of office of the Roman Curia' presented 'reports' to the Synod – some a general view of their work, some on a special theme. Thus Cardinal

Palazzini, Prefect of the Congregation for the Cause of Saints, spoke on 'The Sanctity of the Laity', suggesting that more lay names should be put forward for beatification and canonisation. This led one irreverent colleague to make the outrageous comment: 'Apparently the only good layman is a dead layman'!

A hint, the merest nod, from you-know-whom that journalists may not, in the long run, go home empty-handed: that a summary of proposals may be made available . . . Again, the irreverent (and ungrateful) comment: 'big deal'!

Thursday 29th October

At last we've reached the final working day of the Synod. The Fathers were given the definitive text ('mark' 3) of the proposals last evening, as revised in accordance with such amendments as were accepted (out of 780!). Acceptance depended (apart from duplication of previous contributions) on whether the amendment was consonant with the general thrust of a proposal – if it wasn't, it was thrown out. The decision-makers are those officers of the Synod who had the thankless job of collation: no doubt they will be blamed for the dilution of some of the stronger suggestions. This is a problem neither unique nor easily resolved.

However, voting took place this morning and the results will be announced this evening – though probably not outside the hallowed walls. The names of the new Synod council were announced – they include Archbishop Naidoo of Cape Town, Cardinal Bernardin of Chicago and Cardinal Martini of Milan (among those elected by the Synod) and, perhaps inevitably, Cardinal Ratzinger (nominated with two others by the Pope).

An interesting interlude in this morning's session – if not of immediate synodal relevance – was a statement by Ratzinger on 'the dialogue in progress between the Holy See and Archbishop Lefebvre' – who has apparently agreed to accept an apostolic visitor (named as Cardinal Gagnon), to gather all information required for regularising the situation of Lefebvre's dissident 'Priestly Fraternity of St Pius X'. Cardinal Ratzinger added that 'naturally the hoped for definitive solution is based on the pre-supposition that there exists the obedience due to the supreme pontiff and loyalty to the

Magisterium of the Holy See'. There was apparently no explicit reference to Lefebvre's acceptance of the constitutions and decrees of Vatican II, and of consequent papal instructions – which seems a little curious in view of the fact that his rebellion centred precisely on this . . . Again we'll have to wait and see.

The main item this morning was the presentation to the Synod of the text of a 'Message to the People of God' under the title *In the Path of the Council.*

These 'messages' issued at the end of Synod assemblies are regarded generally as essays in 'cop-out': substitutes for any real information. However, in all fairness, it must be said that their aim is rather different – as we saw at the last 'extraordinary' Synod, when we were also given an account of the statement and proposals put forward to the Pope, and released at his express wish.

The present message will not, I'm afraid, excite any of those members of the people of God who read it: but there are good things in it. Thus:

> As she walks in human history, the Church too must look for new horizons, new challenges . . .

> We condemn the discrimination which proceeds from sin and still continues in our own day in many countries . . .

> If you possess the smallest measure of authority, it is to put yourselves at the service of the human person and not to enslave it . . .

But on the whole, little to stir the blood.

There was thunder today, Roman thunder, as if Jove himself had decided to take a hand, lightning (as advertised on TV), and buckets, or rather continuous vats, of Roman rain. It reminded me that Vatican 1 ended to a similar celestial explosion . . . coupled with Garibaldi's guns, it made some faint hearts wonder if they had been *right*, after all, about infallibility . . . It doesn't appear to have affected today's proceedings except in so far as this poor outsider was trying to keep a date with a Canadian bishop – and was just, quite simply, prevented from doing so by a consortium involvng absent taxi-drivers, the weather people, and of course the curia (with, probably, the active support of *Communione e Liberazione* and all my other enemies). Just because I'm an Irish Catholic.

Anyway I arrived at last, like a drowned rat, at the Sala Stampa for a report on the very last working session. The final vote on the proposals did take place – there are no figures, but I'd be surprised if the results (even if we were given them) contained many or any surprises. The acting president of the session, Cardinal Pironio, delivered himself of some unexceptional thoughts in the manner of a traditional *fervorino* – although he did so following what he saw (and most of us would see) as the triple synodal concern: holiness, communion, mission. He was followed briefly by Pope John Paul.

This afternoon we picked up our copies of the final *sub secreto* version of the Synod proposals, as presented to the Pope. A couple of synodal bishops were there also, seeking to replace the documents they were 'told to hand in'.

And here surely is the biggest let down of the whole month. For it would appear on a rapid run through of the document that the mountain has truly 'conceived, and brought forth a mouse'. The same idea was being freely expressed all round me this evening, by friends of the Church, as well as those not so friendly, but also had been willing to be convinced.

This evening we (the Irish team) went up to the Irish College. The Cardinal and Bishop Daly were quite forthcoming, and the Cardinal for one did not conceal his disappointment over what now is more and more apparently a *non-event* – as far as tangible results are concerned. They both, again, reflected warmly the importance of the synodal *experience,* and the Cardinal was quite lively in defence of the Synod as a collegial institute. But . . .

But as far as hard or clear statements are concerned where are we? Well, certainly, on the question of women in the Church, which the Cardinal raised with great clarity, humour and eloquence (not alone in this Synod, but in the 'extraordinary' one of 1985), there seems to be damn all on offer. He didn't say that, but I doubt if he'd disagree with me.

A suggestion by one of my colleagues that it seemed the Church had 'lost its way' drew Cahal Daly to a vigorous and clearly heartfelt rebuttal: to him, the Synod was an assembly of people from local churches all over the world, determined on bringing the Good News to humanity, with an energy of mind and heart. And, he said, one fundamental fact was made crystal clear: the call to holiness was also a call to the work of justice. To be holy, for priest or layman, could not mean a flight from the human realities, but a dedication to serve and make good in the spirit of the Gospel.

113

Friday 30th October

And so to St Peter's for the closing liturgy. The usual frustrations: tourists taking pictures all over the place, as well as genuine pilgrims who haven't actually planned to spend two hours here – and of course, one's own guilt at looking down the nose at all of these. But, what the hell! It is a celebration of the whole Church . . . well, of the church united with the See of Rome: and the realities of prayer and sacrament shine through . . . Once again, a multi-cultured input: lessons and prayers in Spanish and Creole and Polish and Malay and so on, and of course the omnipresent witness of universality in the great range of race and colour, evident both around the altar and in the whole assembly. The Church may not have yet learned that women could be, and should be, clerics or curial officials or cardinals (to go no further), but, thank God, black and white and yellow can be and are.

The Pope gave a homily, emphasising the three themes of *mystery, communion* and *mission.* He looked back to the 1985 'extraordinary' Synod as providing an introduction to a new understanding of the place of all the people of God in the great *communio* of the Church. He spoke of women and young people, without any particular reference to their roles . . .

After the liturgy, the Synod members were entertained to lunch. I understand that in his informal address to his guests, the Pope said that he 'could understand the annoyance of the journalists' . . . 'Okay,' they say, 'but who allowed it to happen?' – 'it' being the 'secrecy' decision. Was it the group moderators, as we were told? And were Hume and Lorscheider the unlikely chief censors (as *Avvenire* claims)? Or, what? Will we ever know?

This afternoon, the final press conference – again all-star, multilingual. And also, need I say it? – of minimal value to any authentic journalist who has been doing his homework. (Oh! Yes: the 'summary' of the *elenchus* of final draft '3' of the proposals has been made available. Thanks to those responsible – one of whom I believe was Diarmuid. But of course, the full text itself is also 'available'.)

I don't want to sound like a nag, but I have to put it on record that this afternoon's conference was another exercise in futility. Prelates in fancy dress and a tame lay person handing out bland platitudes cannot answer the needs of the media, the church and the world . . .

The hungry sheep look up and are not fed.

Dinner tonight at the Embassy to the Holy See in honour of the Cardinal, as guest of Ambassador Brendan Dillon and his charming wife Alice. I didn't feel it was an occasion to press the Cardinal, but, as last night, he didn't pretend to be over the moon, while still 'enthusiastic' about the Synod process. A pleasant evening, at the end of a none-too-easy month.

The phrase 'love-hate relationship' might have been invented to describe my feelings for Rome. I've been coming here for twenty-five years, and every time I'm charmed, exasperated and moved to something like love. I'm glad that I'm leaving to-morrow morning: this is the first time my wallet has been lost or lifted, and I've had other practical problems. The traffic is awful. Prices have gone up through the roof . And yet, and yet . . .

Saturday 31st October

I'm on BA 503. It's all over and I'm not sure what to say about it. However, to quote the immortal words of Scarlett O'Hara: 'I'll think of that to-morrow' . . . In the meantime, nostalgia is already creeping in.

A rividerci, Roma.

Epilogue

'*I should hope to be surprised*' . . . Well, I wasn't. Not once in the thirty days of the Synod. A little shocked perhaps over the 'secrecy' farce, in that one might reasonably have expected old and very simple lessons to have been learned by now – but not really surprised. It was said of the Bourbons that they learned nothing and forgot nothing. I'm afraid that this great institution in which we serve *does* forget, and learns, if at all, very slowly. I regret I shall have to return once again to the subject of communication (or non-communication), before I hand in these last few pages to my patient publisher, for I do believe the matter is of the essence. But first let us cast an eye on what the thirty days seem to have produced. Concretely there are two documents: the 'Message to the People of God' and the *Elenchus Ultimus Propositionum,* the final list of proposals, as amended, voted on and approved 'by a very large majority'.

This second is, of course, the core document submitted by the Synod to the Pope, as provided for by the synodal regulations, with the expressed hope that its content will contribute to a papal 'exhortation' on 'the Vocation and Mission of the Laity in the Church and the World', to be issued to the universal church 'in due course'. (The last phrase is taken to mean a matter of months.) According to *Avvenire* (which, as the daily voice of *Communione e Liberazione,* must be right!) the Fathers' submission has been accompanied by another text 'of a hundred pages' entitled 'Clarification of the Amendments'. This, we are told, explains to the Pope how the various proposed amendments were dealt with – one criterion for acceptance being, it is said, 'their theological and pastoral validity'. Hmm . . . !

At any rate, all is now presumably on the papal desk, awaiting the attention of one of the world's busiest men. How soon he gets around to it, and how he will deal with it, are matters for, as they say, speculation – a suitable game, perhaps, for the long advent evenings.

In the meantime what can we say? Well even *Avvenire* finds it difficult to suggest that a new era dawns for the people of God. It does its best with headlines, like 'Laity at the frontier of history', a phrase taken from the papal homily at the concluding liturgy, which also spoke of 'an experience without precedent which could become a model, a point of reference for the future'. Predictable, in its own way as *Avvenire,* the headline in *Repubblica* reads 'For the female sex, the altar remains forbidden.' And it quotes Archbishop Weakland as saying: 'The problem, now, is how to go home and explain how the Synod has produced nothing'. (And this is the gentle committed Benedictine who said to me two weeks ago that he was fighting hard to promote the 'extreme centre' . . .) On the last leg of my own journey home, I saw by the *Irish Times* that Cardinal Ó Fiaich said: 'I will go home with renewed enthusiasm and with a need to promote the laity in the church, but I will go home with nothing revolutionary.' And he was 'one of those most disappointed' by the Synod's failure to make some 'big gesture' towards women . . .

The official summary of propositions gives an overall view of the text. A closer look at some of them (in my own 'bootleg' copy) may however be useful. After a brief introduction (propositions 1 and 2), the *first part* of the document seeks to provide a vocational basis for action. Here the theological and ecclesiological approach (propositions 3-5) must be regarded as an improvement on the pre-synodal documents, in emphasising that *all* Christ's faithful, men and women, are of equal dignity as members of God's people in the prophetic, priestly and regal community which is the Church: however lay people participate in this community *especially* through their own secular dimension. (Interestingly, the word 'especially' here was inserted by amendment.) It is also made clear that the laity's 'spiritual life' is essentially *ecclesial,* and also that they too must 'proclaim' Christ in word as well as deed. *Charisms,* or, more simply, gifts of the Holy Spirit 'who breathes as he will', are seen to apply to all the faithful, although their 'discernment' may demand accurate and authoritative criteria.

Part two, concentrating on lay activity within the Church, does so under three headings:

● The diocese and parish (propositions 10, 11)
● Associations and movements (propositions 13-17)

● The 'idea' of ministry (18), lay offices and ministries (19).

The parish is seen as the ordinary structure in which most Catholics gain the experience of 'being church': parish councils and basic communities are ways of promoting a lively cooperation between laity, religious and clerics. Inter-parish and inter-diocesan bodies are also recommended . . . Where priests are few, the parish can maintain its ecclesial character in Sunday worship under lay leadership.

The five proposals on 'associations and movements' reflect recent developments which, in spite of reservations (expressed by several bishops in their interventions), are known to be congenial to the Pope. Two interesting points. In its diocese of origin a movement's authenticity is to be judged by the bishop: if it spreads to other dioceses, the episcopal conference will decide on whether to permit or encourage this: any wider extension of action is for the Holy See to approve. And the propriety of admitting 'non-Catholics' to movements is to be referred in each case to the Pontifical Council for the Laity and to the Secretariat for Christian Unity.

On the subject of lay ministry (19,20), the Synod is extremely cautious, finally passing the question back to the Pope with a suggestion that Paul VI's *Motu Proprio* on 'certain ministries' (1972) should be reconsidered in the light of local usage, especially in relation to the selection of ministerial candidates. An over-liberal appointment of such ministries could obscure the many gifts and functions of the laity in family and civil affairs(!). However it appears that certain forms of lay *munus* (office, function, job) are more welcome: those relating to social and charitable activities in parish and diocese, matrimonial and family affairs, catechesis and other pastoral activities, and administration – where lay competence in financial matters is especially welcome. (This will produce a few wry smiles.)

The bulk of the proposals are in *part three* and are mainly 'secular' in content, or at least in context. The first nine (20-28) deal with political and socio-economic affairs: lay christians are urged to take an active part in bringing the Church's social teaching to the world. Evangelisation, ecumenism, inculturation, secularism, persecution, the new technology, the *media*, account for another nine (29-37): on the whole, there seems little here of *specifically* lay application. 'Popular devotions' and 'the activities of the sects' account for two more (28-39), and lay 'formation' and education generally are dealt with in numbers 40 to 45 – again nothing remarkable.

Then come the two proposals dealing specifically with women: 'Women's special dignity' (46) and 'practical ways of recognising the dignity of women' (47). What do these add up to?

Apart from expressing 'firm' opposition to all forms of 'discrimination and abuse', and deploring discriminatory language, the proposals seem to offer two practical moves: that women should have an equal place with men in administrative and judicial processes in the Church, and that they should be involved in the preparation of pastoral and missionary documents and initiatives. Beyond this the Synod seems unwilling to go – except to propose further anthropological and theological study leading to a definition of 'the true significance and dignity of both sexes'.

Proposals 48 and 52 are concerned with the family and young people, 'not forgetting those who for various reasons do not live within the family ambit *and especially children and young people left to roam the streets and exposed to grave dangers*' (italicised words represent an amendment). The 'sick and sorrowing' are the subject of number 53, with special reference to health-care workers (and their 'formation'). The final proposition invokes the patronage of Mary.

☆

I'm afraid it must be admitted that even the most sympathetic, objective observer will regard such an outcome from thirty days deliberations as very thin gruel. And if my summary may seem unduly sparse, I don't think that the official summary, though wordier and certainly more enthusiastically stated, presents a more nourishing dish. The hungry sheep have at last been fed, but on slender rations . . .

So we seem to be thrown back on the 'process-experience-affective collegiality' argument, as expressed in different ways not just by Pat Jones and Cardinal Ó Fiaich and Gerald O'Collins and Peter Hebblethwaite but by many others, directly or indirectly, officially and informally. I recall Archbishop McGrath of Panama, at a chance encounter at *Pro Mundi Vita:* he saw the Synod as a valuable institution but which needs to get its act together. (His actual words were more dignified, but no less blunt.) He believes that rules and procedures which may have been suitable twenty years ago need radical reform.

Whether in need of reform or not, the value of the Synod process

119

is not, I need hardly say, being seriously advanced as a substitute for more tangible results. Those I have quoted are undoubtedly sincere in their positive evaluation of that process, objectively as well subjectively, and see it as of great, perhaps indispensable, importance to the Church, at this point in post-conciliar history. Undoubtedly any form of collegial activity is better than none – one doesn't have to resort to Chesterton's maxim: 'Anything worth doing is worth doing badly.'

The collegial idea, which excited us all so much twenty-odd years ago, and which seemed destined to give a new face and shape to the magisterium, and to the church's governance in general, does seem to have faded somewhat. Indeed some of us saw the idea as spreading to the diocesan and parish levels, with the bishop, or parish priest, presiding over the representatives of the local church, as the Pope over those of the church universal. It wasn't worked out, but we were sure that it would be, as God's people became more and more actively aware of their mission.

This seemed all the more inevitable as the local churches assumed their autonomous (not, as I've said before, sovereign) roles. There would be a great movement of decentralisation, of 'devolution', which, as inculturation became a real force, would bring a new and vibrant life to the great network of communities, east and west, young and old. And far from this weakening the centre of Catholicity it would lead to a new sense of fraternity, in which unity of faith and love with the bishops of Rome would shine out as a beacon and exemplar in a divided world.

It didn't happen that way. To say that is not to indulge in nostalgia or in speculation over might-have-beens. But one may wish that things were different and legitimately try to make them so. Not all is negative. Thus, the growth of basic communities and the like, rooted in the local church, has been one of the great unforeseen developments of the conciliar era, and has been of incalculable and providential benefit in areas where the institution seemed moribund, and removed from a marginalised, though still believing, people.

Now long accepted, indeed as someone said 'taken for granted', the communities have been, as we have seen, given positive mention in the propositions. Their beneficial activity is by no means confined to the Third World, while some of those nearer home have developed in special ways. Thus the Sant Egidio community in Trastevere in Rome, who work mainly in partnership with the poor, are not confined to the area whose patron they share, although they have many ties with this most attractive, perhaps, of all of Rome's inner-city districts. They were responsible for organising a celebration of prayer for peace during the last week of the Synod, involving christians of all traditions, and representatives of world religions from the Jews to the Zoroastrians: it was centred on the basilica and piazza of Santa Maria in Trastevere, and marked the anniversary of the Pope's inter-faith peace initiative at Assisi last year. What I saw and heard this time was moving, and rang true as a popular enterprise, deeply impressive but without triumphalism.

However the organisational scale of the event led me to ask one of the community's leaders where the money came from. He said it was mostly from popular collections, though they had hopes of some official funding (mainly to cover expenses of visitors). Did he not see the community as becoming dangerously like a movement?! He denied the suggestion and declared they had no territorial ambitions elsewhere. They had become the model for other communities, as far away as the US, but there were no organisational links.

I have perhaps written enough about the movements (especially *Communione e Liberazione*), and am frankly out of sympathy with what I perceive them to be. CL (as it's known) began in a modest way in Milan (as far back as the 50s), and only very slowly developed its rather aggressive present stance and status. Its founder Monsignor Giussani, interviewed in *Avvenire,* expressed satisfaction at the boost given by the Synod, and so well he might. He spoke of their critics more in sorrow than in anger.

No one could deny the potential of such a successful and powerful organisation. Already they have a political wing – the *Movimento Popolare* – and have long outstripped the influence of Italian *Catholic Action,* which deliberately distanced itself some time ago from its own political partners, the Christian Democrats. (It was noticeable that references to the older movement at the Synod tended to be politely reverent . . .) But, as I have indicated, any movement within the Church which achieves a certain degree of 'clout', has established itself internationally, and enjoys papal favour, can be a very mixed blessing indeed. And, in the present context, I can only regard with grave misgivings its 'large-scale' approach, which could all too easily bulldoze small, local growths and impose a centralist, 'cosmopolitan' form of Catholicism, which in the long run can only be a travesty of catholic reality, and of small service to *communio.*

Small, in the church is not only beautiful: it is, quite literally, vital. The world's flowering can come only from the mustard seed. One must then question the collective wisdom of an assembly which, with some outstanding exceptions, seems to have 'bought' the mass-approach. But perhaps it hasn't really. There are undoubtedly many indications that the little cells of which the ecclesial body is made up are also seen as centres of mission and growth.

Cardinal Ó Fiaich regrets the Synod's failure to make one 'big gesture' to women. In this he was by no means alone. Actually, at one stage during the early plenary sessions, women's role was being promoted almost to excess: it seemed unthinkable that the final statement would not include something fairly solid. Were the anti-feminists a silent majority? Or, as has been claimed, did the cultural reservations of a sizeable group (mostly of the Third World) force a withdrawal in the interests of consensus?

The more sober expectations were not in the area of ministry, or not mainly so. It was fairly clear early on that the very concept of lay ministry did not recommend itself to quite a number of the Fathers: in this connection, while the final proposal that Paul VI's *Ministeria Quaedam* should be reviewed is ambiguous in its intent, such a review *might* open non-ordained ministries to women as well as to men (section 7 of the *Motu Proprio* applies). Of course, the ordination of women to the ministerial priesthood could not even be discussed (*nec nominetur . . .!*), while tentative suggestions about their admission to the diaconate were shot down in a shower of scholarly flak.

But it did appear that something substantial might emerge in regard to the structures of government and administration – certainly something more than the rather weak gestures in that direction contained in proposition 47.

It may be argued that far from being gestures, there is considerable substance in this proposal. But even if justice is being done here, it isn't clearly seen to be done. I had some hopes of a general move towards the declericalisation, not of ministry (that would be too much) but of government/administration. In other words, the structures of power. A cynic might say: never!, and, undoubtedly, one doesn't have to imagine the Roman *curia* (or its local equivalents) as being staffed by power-crazed bureaucrats to recognise that those who are used to doing a job, maybe to a point of monopoly, in any society are usually reluctant to hand it over to anyone else. But, in fact, clerical shortages have already led to a laicising of many of the lower ranks, and, with a little collegial pressure, the senior posts might soon follow. After all, as was said in an early session, why does a nuncio or prefect of a congregation have to be a bishop – or in holy orders at all? Why not a layman, or lay woman?

And I must confess that personally I had come around to the view that while, as I have said, the declericalisation of the ordained ministry is not on, for the foreseeable future, a similar declericalisation of the decision-making structures would not alone be an excellent thing in itself (yes! I know the dangers: never mind for the moment), but would inevitably lead to the other, even if later rather than sooner. And, certainly, women as decision-makers could be expected to make more than a few changes, not least in regard to their sisters in, and out of, ministry.

I suppose what, basically, angers women most is precisely having no voice in decisions, most of which affect them to some extent, some very directly indeed – sometimes painfully. I can think of nothing that would do more to remove alienation, and restore their confidence in the institution than a strong, clear indication of practical and immediate moves to remedy this. An unambiguous statement that woman's place is not alone in the home or in the pew but in the Church's government.

Strong, clear, unambiguous. That's how the voice of the Synod should sound to the people of God, and a few short sentences of substance would be worth a hundred pious 'messages' . . . So we're back with communication. Judging by the style and content of this year's effort, those who compose these messages don't seem to have any idea of whom they're addressing. Admittedly it's hard to form a picture of such a vast and disparate body as is made up of Catholics of the world – let alone all those other Christians and people of good-will. But the problem is not a new one: it is, on an admittedly larger scale, that faced by every preacher and every public speaker whose audience is not of one origin, class, educational background. It *is* possible to communicate with a mass audience, and the fact that the great majority of those addressed share a common faith and loyalty must make it a little easier.

However, again on Chesterton's principle, even the woolliest, most pietistic utterance is at least an acknowledgement that there are people out there who, perhaps wrongly, expect to be told about things, and, perhaps even more wrongly, believe they have some right to be told. And yet, in the long run, it is not the institutional church's continuing and repeated failure, apparently, to grasp this elementary point that chiefly causes me dismay. It is because all secrecy, censorship, double-talk and pompous platitude are not just plain silly: they are the very negation of how the Church should act, *because of what the Church is.*

The Church, in Christ, is in the nature of sacrament – *a sign and instrument,* that is, of communion with God and of unity with all men . . .

That's how the Vatican council puts it at the very beginning of *Lumen Gentium.* And it is of course implicit in those two words: 'You are the light of the world' (Matt. 5).

And Jesus went on to point out that a light is meant to bring light. Not to be hidden. To be put where it will do most good . . . We talk of sins against the light, of standing in the way of light – which makes us, whether we realise it or not, agents of darkness.

Since the Church is to be a sign and a light to humanity, it is surely our calling to contribute as we can to the clarity of the sign, the brightness of the light. At the very least, not to get in the way of that brightness, not to obscure it, not to blur the sign. We do these things of course every hour of every day, at least most of us do, when we betray our calling by our behaviour, when we, quite literally, 'put out the light, and then put out the Light'.

But, if our special calling is to be 'special agents' of the light, torchbearers, signwriters – either because of our office or our skills of brain or hand or voice – what then? When we obscure or blur or botch or get in the way, the damage is all the greater.

Worst of all is when we decide that the light may be for us, but not for them. Not under present circumstances. Not without a filter: it might make them blind. Better keep it dark. Keep the sign under wraps.

Put like that, of course, it's all very simple. And I'm not denying that there may be complications at times. But any considered decision to censor, dilute, postpone, conceal, should be taken only for the gravest reasons – like saving lives – and should be a rare exception.

How have the Synod and what has come from it strengthened the Light, made clearer the Sign? What was the effect of whatever news trickled through, including the news about no-news? What impression did the message to the people of God make on the people of God? What do they think of what they have learned of the Synod's submission to the Pope? What do they say to those who praise the 'process' while admitting that little was achieved – or does this make sense at all? How in general do they regard this assembly of a couple of hundred bishops and other church leaders (with a few lay people), which spent a month discussing *them* and telling them, in the end, very little?

These are not rhetorical questions, and I don't know the answers, though I can make an educated guess at a few of them. In the course of my Diary I have referred (rather sourly) to one or two occasions of synodal communication as 'non-events'. On reflection, I cannot honestly find in me to withdraw the comment. And, equally honestly, I have to say that the whole Synod seems to have been so regarded by most people I've spoken to, in Rome and here in Dublin. If this is an unfair judgement, or at least an inadequate one, who is to blame for it? Certainly not those (given their honesty and goodwill, which I would confirm) who have made the judgement. They can only go on what they have been told, what they have learned, what – in a few cases – they've gone to some trouble to find out.

Once again, communication is the problem. A problem for us, the plain people who are at the receiving (or non-receiving) end: but, far more seriously, a problem for church authority and 'leadership'. And most seriously of all because it isn't perceived to be a problem – or, at least, one of any great importance. It seems to be something like a blind spot . . . May I cite a parallel?

At Mass, in all too many churches, the proclamation of the word suffers all too often from a serious lack of intelligibility and even audibility. Bad reading, bad diction, misuse or abuse of microphones. Now, here is something of the first importance in the liturgical life of God's people . . . they come to hear, and too often are left straining their ears. But I'm afraid that as often as not, while this is regarded as unfortunate, and something of a flaw in the celebration, it's not *really* seen as serious – not as serious say, as omitting part of the eucharistic prayer, or forgetting to put water in the wine – or even leaving the candles unlit. *Opus operatum* may not still rule OK, but its influence lingers on.

I would suggest that something of the same mentality accounts, at least partly, for the failure to communicate on other levels – and the failure to see that such failure touches the very core of what the Church is for and should be about. We recognise the fundamental, indeed the primal, importance of *mission* as a *sine qua non* in the life of God's people. But what is mission without communication?

And if we have begun to recognise that mission, like charity, it must begin at home, and that everything we say and do within the Church and outside it has, for good or ill, a missionary connotation, how can we be so insensitive to the effect of the Church's proceedings and statements, so careless of the *image* they project? I am far from proposing that we should engage in 'creating' a new image, or in polishing and sanitising the old ones. I am not using the word image in its customary PR sense, which has too often little to do with the reality it's meant to 'sell'.

Our concern is with *telling the truth in love*, not selling anything. The Synod of bishops is an expression of church life, of recent origin and, one might say, experimental structure. What it does and says may be of no great interest to the world, but it is of some interest, and could be of some value, to some people all over the world, not all of them Catholics. And to this end, they must be seen and heard as they are, warts and all. Above all, let no well-meaning intermediary try to rub off the corners, remove the rough edges and convey an impression not only of unity but of *uniformity*.

One of the factors that seriously reduces the credibility of the present Synod is the absence of conflict or, at least, of any serious differences of opinion as published. To admit that such exist would no doubt be deemed 'imprudent', and bordering on scandal, by some of those in a position to influence such matters. In fact, the real scandal consists in presenting a bland and unremittingly uniform face to the world – a face that surely must be a facade, if, that is, the Synod is actually a living thing. For where there is life there is conflict: not necessarily involving violence or hostility, but honest and open.

It is, indeed, sometimes alleged (and this year's assembly was no exception) that the very nature and status of the Synod tends to discourage the expression of strongly opposed views – especially where these are regarded as of a 'minority', with implications of eccentricity, 'unsoundness', or perhaps near-heresy. I have even heard it suggested – though this can hardly be true – that ideas (even on 'doubtful' or 'open' questions) which the Pope is known not to favour are regarded as unsuitable for discussion.

But rumours like these, as I have said so often, are the predictable spawn of the kind of darkness which the secrecy sickness engenders. And, indeed, of the whole failure of the institutional church to come to terms with a world where people want to know, and expect to be told even when they don't. This is not an aspect of secularisation, or of middle-class trendiness, or intellectual hedonism or any of the other maladies to which we are allegedly subject. The Church's duty to communicate is rooted, as I've tried to say, in her founder's command and charge.

Eppur si muove. The people of God, men and women, old and young, ordained and married and celibate, are still in pilgrimage. Our journey is, among other things, one of self-discovery, and, however slowly, we are learning all the time – about ministry and sexuality and community and mission and culture and the whole story of the earth, of this world we live in. Some of us are learning more quickly than others, but the slow learners may stay the course better.

The gain from this bit of the pilgrimage may seem hardly worth the labour. I must say that's how I've been feeling myself. But maybe I'll still be surprised – after the event. Maybe we all will. There's always hope.

Féile Naomh Uile Éireann 1987.